BELIEVER IN BLUE

MARVIN ANDREWS

BELIEVER IN BLUE

MARVIN ANDREWS

Football, My Life, My Faith

With David Mason

Foreword by Barry Ferguson

pitch

First published by Pitch Publishing, 2025
Reprinted 2025
2

Pitch Publishing
9 Donnington Park,
85 Birdham Road,
Chichester, West Sussex,
PO20 7AJ

www.pitchpublishing.co.uk
info@pitchpublishing.co.uk

A CIP catalogue record is available for this book from the British Library.

ISBN 978-1-83680-224-2

Typesetting and origination by Pitch Publishing

MIX
Paper | Supporting responsible forestry
FSC™ C016779

Printed and bound in the UK on FSC® certified paper in line with our continuing commitment to ethical business practices, sustainability and the environment.

Printed and bound in India by Replika Press Pvt. Ltd.

Contents

DEDICATION

To my grandmother, Isidora Rose Andrews, who loved and cared for me and placed me on a path of righteousness and faith in the Lord Jesus Christ.

Acknowledgements

ALEX McLEISH, Jimmy Nicholl, Barry Ferguson, Bob Malcolm, Terry Butcher, Gordon Chisholm and Scott Thomson for their contributions. David Mason for his guidance in the preparation of this book. Pastor Joe Nwokoye for his help on my spiritual journey with the Lord Jesus Christ. Pitch Publishing for helping the whole thing come to fruition. Also, I used, for reference, my autobiographical account *Marvellous Marvin – The Life, Football, and Faith of a Soca Warrior*, first published in 2007 by Mainstream Publishing Company (Edinburgh) Ltd.

DAVID MASON

David has been official club historian of Rangers Football Club since 1986. He has written several books on the club and some of its important personalities, including: the 150th anniversary edition of *The Official Rangers Story*; *Mr Struth: The Boss*, *Rangers: The Managers*, *A Match to Remember;* and *The Penalty King.* He has also written features in the Rangers matchday programme for some time and has appeared on TV and radio, relating aspects of the club's history. Through these connections, David has known Marvin for many years, firstly as a player and now as a colleague, working in Rangers' corporate hospitality.

Foreword by Barry Ferguson

Former captain of Rangers Football Club

Barry Ferguson played a total of 482 times for Rangers, scoring 73 goals in an Ibrox career that spanned 13 seasons. His honours with the club include five league championships, five Scottish Cups and five League Cups. He also captained the side to the domestic treble in season 2002/03. Considered one of the finest midfielders to play for Rangers, he earned 45 caps for Scotland and in 2004, at just 26, he was inducted into the club's prestigious Hall of Fame. A former team-mate, Barry has seen Marvin experience highs and lows in his Rangers career and reach a pinnacle of success in the 2004/05 championship win, famed for its drama on what has been called 'Helicopter Sunday'.

MARVIN ANDREWS – what a brilliant guy! I was really delighted, for several reasons, when he asked me to write this foreword for him. He is a good friend and has remained so ever since we first played at Rangers together 20 years ago. This foreword gave me a chance to express my thoughts on this wonderful character who never fails to put a smile on my face.

I must concede that when I first heard back in 2004 that Rangers would sign Marvin, I was underwhelmed. I was still at Blackburn Rovers at the time, but events at Ibrox were never far from my mind. Rangers' football was about quick passing, the pass and move game which I did not think was suited to Marvin's style. I knew that he was magnificent in the air but that his strength was not on the ground. I need not have worried. He settled into Ibrox immediately and I quickly realised what a shrewd decision Alex McLeish had made when he brought him to the club.

When I rejoined the club several months later, I could see at first-hand what a valuable member of the team he was. Marvin fitted in so easily to our side because he kept things simple. It was seamless and we had acquired a real colossus of a man. He never tried to be something that he was not and instead of launching big crossfield passes, he just won the ball then moved it on to us. In fact, he was so strong aerially, he could head that ball further than he could pass it!

With his bubbly character, Marvin took no time at all in settling in amongst the boys. Indeed, just after he arrived, you would have thought he had been there for years. Besides being immediately popular in the dressing room, we quickly saw what an excellent defender he was. I loved his spirit. He was the kind of player who wore his heart on his sleeve and put his body on the line in every game. When there was a ball to be won in the air or on the ground, there was no one more committed. Nothing would deter him and it was dangerous to even be in the vicinity when he was in full flight! Even I suffered on occasions when he powered through to win the ball. Often playing just in front of him, I got four or five bumps on the head to verify his commitment. I even came away with a broken nose in training once, when we played five against two in a small box!

We did not need much convincing of his value in terms of the strength he provided, but he offered much more than that physicality to the team. He has always been such a positive character and that was never so valuable than on 'Helicopter Sunday'. The week leading up to the game was difficult for the players because there was an expectation that Celtic would go on and win the Scottish Premier League. No one gave us a chance and we had doubts, too. However, Marvin lifted us with his constant message of 'keep believing' and, although we might not have been convinced, he was right. He was such a calming influence on the team going into the game. That was so important, and then, of course, when the events unfolded, it was not so much a case of reflecting on our own faith – we all looked at Marvin as if he was God!

We all knew about Marvin's faith before he came to Ibrox and we embraced him. Today, he is still the same guy we saw when he first walked into Murray Park – a man who is so full of happiness that it is infectious when you are with him. He never changed my outlook as he might have suggested. I still like a moan, as I always did, but he certainly altered my outlook on life. I would let defeat fester and if we lost a crucial game, it was like the end of the world to me, but I am more reflective now. I still hate losing, but I have come to realise that there is nothing you can do when the game is in the past.

I had some tough times personally when Paul Le Guen arrived as Rangers manager and in having to deal with media stories suggesting that I was at the centre of a clique at Ibrox at the time. It was total nonsense, which everyone around the club knew and so did Marv. I was down about the whole affair but Marvin, in particular, stuck with me and was a great friend through that period. We constantly exchanged calls and messages, which helped hugely. When I was left out of the squad, he remained positive, telling me that I would be back in the side and not to be down. It all unravelled and I did get my place back, of course, and Marvin was one of the guys who had offered me the greatest support. I owe him a great deal of gratitude for that.

When he was nearing the end of his contract, I signed him for Clyde when I was manager there. He was such an important signing for me because I knew he would be a huge influence on the team and the dressing room. All the players looked up to him and loved him. He was such a big character that you could hear his voice and that daft laugh of his 100 yards from the dressing room. Then there was his endless singing! Always a lively character, he really lifted that place and, importantly, on the field I could always rely on him, away from all the fun. Even when I occasionally left him out, simply because we had games in quick succession, he never allowed his disappointment to affect his support for the team. There was no chance he would ever spit out the dummy! He would always be in there rallying the other guys. After I left the club, he decided to move on too, but what a wonderful service he provided to Clyde and to me over that period.

Nowadays, I see Marvin quite often around Ibrox as we help out in hospitality. As always when we meet, I emerge with a smile on my face, reflecting his own. He has that effect on people. Let us not forget what a wonderful player he was at Ibrox in that brief period, culminating in 'Helicopter Sunday'. Certainly, he is a Rangers hero, but he is more than that to me. He is a great friend and always will be.

Chapter One

'The Helicopter Is Changing Direction'

A PLAYER'S football career is rarely defined by one match, but I will always be remembered for the events of 22 May 2005, at least by the fans of Rangers FC. Rarely a week passes when I am not reminded of that pivotal moment in my life, when the club won the Scottish Premier League championship after few had given the team an earthly chance. That very special and fateful game took place at Hibernian's Easter Road stadium in Edinburgh. The day would be forever known as 'Helicopter Sunday'.

By then, I had already reached some important footballing milestones in my career, having played for the Trinidad and Tobago international side and gone on to represent them in World Cup qualifying matches. I had also helped Livingston achieve the greatest result in their history when they won the Scottish League Cup. However, no matter how significant these events had been in my career, nothing compared to that day in Scotland's capital when a quite remarkable change of fortune unfolded over a glorious afternoon in the Edinburgh sunshine.

The drama had started for me eight weeks earlier, on 13 March 2005, when I sustained an injury in an important league match against Dundee at Dens Park. In the closing stages, I suffered an injury to my left knee that I knew was bad as soon as I was hurt in a challenge with Dundee's Steve Lovell. As we collided, he came down on top of my leg, forcing it to bend backwards.

I limped off the field and, when I got back to Glasgow, I was subjected to intensive and detailed medical examinations. The doctor and physios at Ibrox diagnosed a torn anterior cruciate ligament. More commonly referred to as the ACL, it is one of the ligaments inside your knee that joins the thigh bone (femur) to the front of the shin bone (tibia). The medical opinion was not encouraging, so Rangers referred me to external specialists to see what could be done. In fact, I would eventually go to see three consultants and had scans with each – two in Glasgow and one in England.

The specialists I visited in England had also been involved in the examination and treatment of similar injuries sustained by Paul Gascoigne and Alan Shearer. They were the best in the business. The news following all the assessments was not good. I was told that I would need surgery, with a lengthy period of rehabilitation afterwards. It was suggested that I could be out of football for nine months, which would effectively end my season at the most crucial stage. In fact, going with their prognosis, it would be well into the next season before I would be ready. With only two years left on my contract at the season's end, it could even mean the end of my career at Rangers.

One match that I was certain to miss was the Scottish League Cup Final, which was due to be played the following week against Motherwell. It was a huge disappointment, especially since that tournament had brought me much joy when I won it with Livingston the previous season. I had to set that aside, because now it was all about getting fit again. A chance of a first medal with Rangers had gone. I could only watch from afar as the team went on to beat Motherwell 5-1, with Bob Malcolm taking my place in the defence.

I would also miss crucial World Cup qualifying matches as Trinidad and Tobago pursued a much-coveted place at the 2006 finals to be held in Germany.

Everyone in Scottish football knew that I had strong faith, but they were probably unprepared for the judgement I made in the aftermath of these medical opinions. I reported the specialists' advice to the medical team back at Ibrox, but I told them that God would heal my knee. I had considered what the doctors said, but I believed that my faith in God would see me through without resorting to such radical intrusive treatment. I had experienced the power of faith in healing not long after I joined Raith Rovers in 1997 when I was diagnosed with an inflamed pelvis. The doctors said I would not be able to play again unless I had surgery. The procedure they recommended involved scraping away the inflammation and then an operation to insert a metal plate inside me. I was not going to do that, as I was convinced that it was not God's plan. I did not believe God created me to have a metallic plate inserted in my stomach!

I spoke with one of my Trinidadian team-mates, Anthony Rougier. He had come to Scotland in 1995 and signed with Raith Rovers, going on to help them win the Scottish First Division title in 1994/95. He had made such an impact in Scottish football that he was signed by Scottish Premier League side Hibernian in July 1997 for a £250,000 fee. His departure had come just a few months before my arrival in Scotland, so I never got the chance to meet and play with him at Stark's Park. However, we knew each other from playing with the international side, although he was more of a casual acquaintance at that time, rather than a close friend. He still lived in Kirkcaldy when I arrived, which gave me the chance to get to know him better.

I spoke to Anthony about my injury problem and he suggested I come to his church. Like me, he was also Christian and was a strong advocate of faith healing. He invited me to meet Pastor Joe Nwokoye, a Nigerian who had come to the UK in 1986 and established the Zion Praise Centre in Kirkcaldy.

Pastor Joe had held healing services and told me that God would heal me. While I was a believer, I had not experienced that purpose and power of belief before. I felt that I had nothing to lose by attending and hearing what Pastor Joe had to say. He directed me to parts of the Bible where Jesus had healed the sick, restored sight in a blind man and performed other miracles. I had nothing to lose. The alternative was an operation. I prayed with him, then continued my own prayers. I found it edifying as we prayed together and I went on to pray with him almost every day. Gradually, the pain and problems with my injury subsided, so much so that I could resume playing.

The whole experience was enlightening for me. After going to Pastor Joe, my eyes were opened to the power of faith, especially in healing, and that strengthened my own faith in God. I had been brought up to believe in God from my childhood and I was already praying twice a day. The experience of my healing through the visits to the Zion Praise Centre had reaffirmed my beliefs in God, but also showed another aspect to faith that I had not explored previously. I know that God healed me. After I returned to the Raith Rovers team, that 1998/99 season turned out to be a fantastic one for me. Although Anthony had moved on to Hibernian from Raith Rovers, our relationship continued to strengthen. I would often be invited to dinner with him and his wife and even today we keep in close contact, although he now lives in the United States.

Back at Ibrox, it would be fair to say that my decision to rely on faith rather than embarking on surgery caused some angst and surprise within the club. I still have the letter that Mr Paul Rae, the specialist surgeon who examined my knee, had written. He wrote that I had suffered an acute injury to the ACL and, critically, he added: 'I think this is a significant injury and I would advise against trying to play or train.' He was aware that I was averse to the operation he was proposing and he wrote: 'Ultimately, the decision does rest with Marvin, but I think it should be emphasised that there is a risk of severely aggravating the knee and making things worse.'

I am sure that these comments spooked the Rangers backroom staff. They were convinced that their medical advice was sound and that there was no way that I would be able to continue without going under the knife. They were so astonished, in fact, that they felt it necessary to put out a press statement, possibly partly to ensure that they were covered from an insurance viewpoint. After all, they were simply following the advice of the specialist who had advised me against playing or training. The statement read: 'Marvin Andrews sustained cruciate ligament damage to his left knee in the game against Dundee on Sunday, 13 March. It is the medical opinion that he needs an operation. Marvin fully understands the advice he has been given, however he has declared himself fit and wishes to continue training and playing.'

I had a meeting with David Murray, chief executive Martin Bain, Alex McLeish, the medical staff and various other Rangers executives. The meeting was to discuss my whole injury situation and my decision. McLeish said after the meeting: 'We just wanted to let you know that, based on you rejecting our advice from the medical standpoint, we'd like to give you a disclaimer that you sign so that you take full responsibility if anything goes wrong with your knee from here on out.' The club reasoned that signing the disclaimer would mean I could not sue Rangers or make the club pay for my decision in any way if I damaged my knee or my knee collapsed in training or wherever. With the faith that I had in God, I said: 'No problem, I will trust God that he will look after me.' So, I signed the disclaimer and took full responsibility for any consequences of a collapse of my knee. There were risks, of course. A lot of people do not know that when I was playing for Rangers after the injury, I was not covered by the club's insurance. My insurance came from God.

The Rangers medical staff remained unconvinced that I could possibly recover and play before the season was out. Since I was injured, I could not train with the first-team squad at first and went through various physical tests and a rehabilitation programme under the watchful eye of the Ibrox doctor, Ian McGuinness. These tests were to assess how practical it was for me to join in sessions with the rest of the squad. He had me doing various exercises, all putting pressure on my knee, like jumping on one leg to test its strength. Everything was geared towards assessing the condition of my knee and whether it would stand up to action on a football field.

I should add that I do not criticise the specialists and medical team at Ibrox in any way. I respect these highly trained people for the work they do. They have been blessed with the skills to help people. However, I just saw it differently and I did not feel it was God's will for me to go under the knife at that time.

When I came through these tests and rehabilitation, and convinced the staff that I was recovering, they reintroduced me to training with the first-team group and closed-door matches with my team-mates at Murray Park. These games were still somewhat artificial in that the players obviously knew of my knee issues and might have held back a little in the tackle. However, shortly afterwards, a game was arranged against Clyde at Broadwood Stadium. That was a real test for my knee and I came through it unscathed. By then, I think, Alex McLeish realised that I had returned to fitness and that perhaps I would be available for the crucial league run-in after all, although I am sure he and his staff still had doubts about my knee.

Alex McLeish (Manager of Rangers FC) – *Our advice was that he needed an operation and even if he declared himself fit (as he did eventually), we thought that from a moral point of view it was important from* *his perspective that he got an operation. We didn't want him breaking down, but he said to me, 'I am taking that responsibility.'*

In my absence, the team had looked a bit vulnerable at the back, especially when we lost to bottom-of-the-table Dundee United at Ibrox on 12 April 2006. With that defeat, we surrendered our lead in the championship with just six games to go in the title race. Celtic had overtaken us and we were due to face them on 24 April 2006. It would be one of those must-win situations in which a defeat could effectively end our hopes. The manager knew he had a decision to make, since I was brought in particularly to combat the physical presence of the Celtic frontmen, most notably the burly John Hartson. If McLeish was ever going to take a chance in bringing me into a game, it had to be this one. He wanted my physicality and that was why I was at Ibrox.

The press speculation that I could return to the side was rife. McLeish conceded to the press that I was training as hard as ever, but it was not clear that I would be considered ready to return. I had not played for almost six weeks and the manager almost certainly considered that match fitness, quite apart from physical fitness, was an issue. However, I felt fit and eager to play. I had been subjected to rigorous tests from the physios, examining my knee to determine whether it would stand up. It seemed fine but, as McLeish highlighted to me, none of all that physical testing and training could replicate the conditions I would experience in the match.

I knew he was concerned that if he selected me and it did not work out, his plans for the game would have been disrupted. I felt ready for it and was desperate to get back on the field, but I thought that the best that I could hope for would be a place on the bench. All that week, the media speculation continued over whether I would play. They all offered comment on the attributes I could bring for this game, highlighting the challenge I could add to Celtic's physical presence. Some also spoke about my value at set pieces, with my strength in the air. I would not know McLeish's decision until the day of the match. That was the protocol, as the manager usually revealed his team after we had lunch in the Cooper Suite at Ibrox.

On matchday, with the tension already building, we gathered inside Ibrox for lunch. Afterwards, we headed down the marble staircase and along the corridor to the dressing room. I sat down in my usual place on the bench just inside the door and, with an hour until kick-off, we were all anxious to find out who would be playing. The manager came in and proceeded to use a flip chart, flicking over the top sheet to reveal his team. I immediately saw my name. There was no need to speculate any more – I was playing. I was nervous, not just because we were facing our biggest rivals, but because it seemed such a long time since I last featured in a game. In training, I had not experienced any pain in my knee, so I was sure it would be fine and would stand up to the rigours of an Old Firm clash, which was invariably physical. However, I realised that all eyes would be on me.

We came out of the tunnel to the usual incredible atmosphere of the Old Firm match, with both sets of supporters singing and chanting. Every match is important, but this one seemed especially so because there were only five games left in the title race. It was the first time in my life that I felt I had a camera follow me as I came on to the field and for the whole time I was on the pitch.

I had joined the rest of the team on the field for the warm-up before the sides were read out in the stadium, so the fans knew I was in the frame to play. The game kicked off with the usual deafening noise coming from all around the stands. After a few early exchanges in the opening minutes, I went in for a challenge with Celtic's Craig Bellamy and I felt my knee jarring. Many people inside the ground were no doubt anxiously watching to see if my knee would collapse. I didn't go down, but I felt the intense pain and tried to run it off. I kept praying to God to help me through the match and gradually it eased.

We had a poor first half and lost two goals before rallying after the break. I felt I could have done more to stop Stan Petrov open the scoring. I was ring rusty and did not have the sharpness to close him down, but none of that was down to my knee. We rallied a bit in the second half. I hit the bar late on as we pushed to get back in the game, but it wasn't to be. I felt fine throughout the game, but was substituted after 83 minutes. It was not through the injury, but because I was tiring. We managed to pull a goal back near the end through Steven Thompson, but we could not get the equaliser. Despite us going down 2-1, it was generally agreed that I played well for my level of fitness, considering how long I had been out. Regardless, it was not the result that many felt we needed.

My knee had stood up to the most rigorous of challenges. Some suggested it was the strength of my quad muscles that provided support to my knee, providing compensation for the problems with my ACL. Perhaps so, but these are the muscles God gave me.

The result against Celtic put them into a strong position in the championship, with a five-point lead. Assuming we won all our matches, they only needed to win three of their last four games to seal the title. Barry Ferguson said in the post-match interviews that we had little chance of winning the title and most of our players now doubted that we could win the championship. Everyone else, too, was writing us off, but I was interviewed afterwards and told the media: 'Keep believing! It's not over until God says it's over.' Almost every day I went into Murray Park for training, my team-mates would ask: 'Are you sure we're going to win the league, Marvin?' I replied: 'Yes, guys, keep believing.' Some said they would come to my church if we won the title!

All we could do thereafter was keep winning games and hope that Celtic would falter. We had a difficult match at Pittodrie against Aberdeen the following week, but we were thrown a lifeline 24 hours before that game when Celtic surrendered a chunk of their lead by losing 3-1 to Hibernian. Ironically, the third and clinching goal for the Edinburgh side was scored by Scott Brown, who would go on to become a star with the Parkhead side.

The next day, we travelled to Pittodrie, which had traditionally been a difficult place for us to visit. Celtic's defeat put an extra spring in our step, but the match worried me because the pitch was sodden. Even Alex McLeish stepped in to ask Aberdeen to drain it at half-time, as the weather threatened an abandonment of the game. It was not ideal for our type of game, or for me if my knee was suspect, but there were no problems. We managed to win 3-1, with two-goal Dado Prso our hero. I was also singled out for praise by Dons boss Jimmy Calderwood. We played well and the victory was comfortable, especially coming off the back of that Old Firm defeat.

The game was marred somewhat by an incident when Fernando was hit by a coin when taking a corner. Our players had been pelted with objects any time we went near the Dons fans. Fernando had been hit earlier in the season at Celtic Park and this time he called on the authorities to take strong action for the safety of players. The fixture with Aberdeen at Pittodrie had long been a cauldron of hate. Whenever I played them at their ground while with Livingston, I never endured any problems from the home crowd. But an indication of their antipathy with anything connected with Rangers came when I went back up to Pittodrie with Livi just after it was announced I would join the Ibrox club at the end of the season. I was barracked as if I already had a blue jersey on my back and not a Livingston one.

The win over Aberdeen put us within two points of Celtic and now we had a chance, although a slender one. We kept plugging away and another two good wins, against Hearts at Tynecastle and then Motherwell at Ibrox, kept us within touching range of our rivals. Ironically, I scored own goals in each of those games, although I could do little to avoid the first of them when our keeper, Ronald Waterreus, fumbled a cross. The second one came after I had doubled our lead against Hearts. In the dying minutes, I diverted a free kick that slipped past our keeper. Neither mattered and the points were ours.

Despite those wins and us showing some good form against both Hearts and Motherwell, most remained sceptical that we could win the title. It would all come down to that final day of the championship race on 22 May 2005. By the end of the day, the winners would be celebrating and the cup, draped with ribbons in the colours of the champions, would be presented to the captain. Just a few weeks earlier, it seemed that our chance had gone. We had now closed to within two points of Celtic, but those who retained some faith that we could go on and win the title were few and far between.

Our final match would be in Edinburgh against Hibernian. What was certain was that we could not win the championship if we did not win that final game. That had to be our focus. Meanwhile, all Celtic had to do was win at Motherwell to guarantee the title. The Fir Park side had not performed well against Rangers in losing the League Cup Final 5-1 the week after I sustained my injury. We had beaten them 4-1 just a week before Celtic would go to Fir Park and they also had a number of key players missing. The drama of the final-day shoot-out was built up by the media and both our match and that of our Parkhead rivals would be broadcast live. The simultaneous transmissions would give fans the chance to keep in touch with the events at both grounds that would seal the destiny of the trophy. The authorities had arranged for a helicopter to deliver the trophy to Fir Park or Easter Road so it could be presented on the field to the champions. Most expected it would be flying to Motherwell.

The title was Celtic's to win, but also to lose, although that seemed unlikely. Surely they would get the victory that would give them the championship. We were determined to go all out for a win just in case there was a surprise at Fir Park. We had already beaten Hibs three times that season, but this was different and nothing before would matter if we failed to take the points on this occasion. Of course, the Edinburgh side were confident they could turn us over, having beaten Celtic at Parkhead. They had an extra incentive for the game. They held a narrow goal-difference lead over Aberdeen in the chase for a UEFA Cup place.

I sensed that many of our team were not confident that we could win the title. We had travelled to Edinburgh the day before, staying at the Hilton hotel at Edinburgh Airport. We would normally have stayed at the Marriott, which was more expensive, but there was a bit of cost-cutting by the club and that probably gives some indication of how the directors thought the day might end. The atmosphere amongst the team was subdued. Many were anxious and worried about what seemed the inevitable outcome. There was a realisation and fear that even if we got a victory against Hibernian, it could all be in vain. In that old football cliché, it could be 'so near, yet so far'. Some of our players were far from motivated to play. It is difficult playing a dead rubber when your rivals are enjoying the prospect of drinking champagne.

Manager McLeish sensed he had to lift the players and said to us: 'Regardless of the outcome at Motherwell, the one thing you cannot do is fail to win this game. If, for some reason, Celtic drop points and you don't do your jobs and win the game, you will regret it for the rest of your lives. You will wake up in the middle of the night with cold sweats.'

He wanted to make sure that we did all that was necessary at Easter Road and told us: 'If it's not to be, then we can say it was a great effort and we will still be hailed as a great team for only just losing out.' He stressed again that we had to make sure we won the game.

If our team wasn't exactly brimming with confidence, the sentiments were shared by a fair proportion of our fans, who also carried a bit of negativity. Just a week earlier at Ibrox in our penultimate game, some had seized upon the comments I had made urging them to 'keep believing' and had unfurled a banner with these words but that optimism appeared thin on the ground at Easter Road. Perhaps they were preparing for the likely disappointment, but it seemed that there were a few spaces in the Hibs ground, when normally it would have been packed to capacity in the south stand where our fans were traditionally allocated.

The strength of my beliefs told me that this was the perfect stage for God to perform a miracle. I told my team-mates exactly that as they sat in the dressing room before the match. I even wore a T-shirt with the following words written on the chest: 'The things that are impossible with men are possible with God.' It was taken from the Bible, Luke 18:27, and seemed so appropriate here. I wore it under my jersey that day. Everything had been set up for God to perform a miracle.

I had collected several T-shirts with different quotes from the Bible and always wore one of these beneath my club jersey. I got them made myself, ordered from a small shop in Kirkcaldy. If I scored a goal in a match, I would reveal the message for the day. On that day at Easter Road, I decided on that specific T-shirt because the words in the scripture were so appropriate to the circumstances.

As we came on to the field for our day of destiny, led out by captain Fernando Ricksen, we received the usual tremendous welcome from our travelling fans and ran to applaud them. We had to dismiss from our minds any thoughts of the events unfolding at Fir Park. Our fans, many of whom seemed to have radios, would surely keep us informed of any important developments.

As the game kicked off, we were on the attack from the beginning, but things weren't happening for us. We just couldn't make the breakthrough and the first half seemed to drift past without incident and remained goalless. The fans had been quiet and we sensed that things were not going our way in Motherwell, so we did not expect good news when we came off the park and headed back to our dressing room. The backroom guys confirmed that Celtic were a goal up, which did not help the general mood. Again, there was that despondency, but I later learned that McLeish had pulled a particularly low Barry Ferguson aside and told him: 'You can't be sitting there with your face tripping you. You've got to be rallying these guys.'

Barry was a dyed-in-the-wool Rangers fan and hated losing. His reaction to the half-time situation was inevitable and he couldn't hide the depth of his disappointment. I knew that I also had to do my bit to lighten the mood, so I went around telling everyone: 'Keep believing, keep believing.'

Alex McLeish (Former Rangers Manager) – *Marvin was hugely important to us in the lead-up to that match at Easter Road and also at half-time when others were a bit despondent. He is very much a 'glass half full' type of guy and I needed that to lift the players. I had lifted Barry Ferguson and told him I needed him to rally the players, which he took on board and responded by becoming very vocal with them. At the same time, Marvin was going around them all telling them to 'keep believing' and urging them on for the second half. I explained the importance of a win and told them they had to up the tempo of the game. The boys certainly responded, going on to get the win that was so vital to us.*

The manager said that if we scored a goal and Motherwell got an equaliser, we would be champions. It was that simple. To many, it appeared fanciful, but it gave everyone a lift and we went out with a spring in our step and a little more urgency. There was nothing we could do but focus on our own match and that is what we set out to do.

The breakthrough in our game finally came with the goal we desperately needed. Thomas Buffel, who had missed an earlier chance, made amends by putting Nacho

Novo through after 59 minutes. The little Spaniard did what he excelled at, sneaking goals, as his effort deflected in off Gary Caldwell. The match then entered a weird phase. Hibs would qualify for Europe if they did not lose heavily and, of course, we had the result we needed. So, both teams sat back, content with what they had. We knew that if we did not do anything stupid, the game and the points would be ours.

At one stage in the match, things opened up in front of me and I had a chance to break forward. As I galloped through the middle, I could hear the bellowing voices of McLeish and Alex Rae telling me to get back. I moved the ball along and returned to my central defensive position alongside Soti Kyrgiakos. There would be no more venturing over the halfway line for me.

From there, we were essentially playing out time, waiting, hoping and, in my case, praying that God would turn things our way. It was all rather surreal. Hibs hardly ventured forward and we were also content to retain possession, keeping things tight and holding on to what we had. Then, with just a few minutes remaining, there was an almighty cheer from our fans. We knew immediately that Motherwell had scored. The delight surged throughout our team, as we could hardly believe what was happening. With the excitement building at the end, I kept praying that we would not make a mistake at the back that could unravel the whole situation. We didn't! Then, a minute or so later, there was another massive roar. We thought that the game had finished at Fir Park with the 1-1 result which would have been enough for us, but it turned out Motherwell had scored again through Scott McDonald. It was 2-1 and there was no way back for Celtic. We would be crowned champions.

I thought to myself: 'Lord Almighty – you are so wonderful!'

When we had learned at half-time that Celtic were leading, we had thought the title was over, but it wasn't! I can't thank God enough for the miracle that he provided for me. I could not believe what was happening when we later heard that Motherwell had scored not just once, but twice. I remember Barry Ferguson jumping on Alex Rae's back with delight while Hibs still had the ball!

It was quite ironic that Gary Caldwell, who deflected the ball for our goal, and Scott McDonald, who scored these two vital Motherwell goals, would eventually end up with Celtic. Here they were playing such a big part in the events that turned the title our way.

After the final whistle, I dropped to my knees and looked skywards to thank God. It is an image that many people remember after it was captured by some press photographers. We were surrounded by our fans, who came on to the field to join us in celebration. The first one who came to me was in tears and said: 'I just love you so much. I believe, I believe!'

I then joined the rest of the players and we partied on the field while up in the sky, the helicopter that was once on its way to Fir Park with the trophy bedecked in green and white ribbons was rerouted to Easter Road. The ribbons were changed and were now red, white and blue. When it landed in the middle of the pitch, everyone in blue was ecstatic. What seemed so unlikely just 45 minutes earlier had come true. Not even our most fervent fan, kit man Jimmy Bell, expected it. He hadn't packed any champagne and we had to borrow some from Hibs, who had their own celebrations over the European place they had sealed.

Bob Malcolm (Team-mate at Rangers FC) – *Looking back on that fantastic time, Marvin's influence on us was so important. He was always jovial and positive in the dressing room and that began to rub off on us. Few of us believed that we could win the championship that day and most of the players felt that the game at Easter Road was a pointless rubber on a day when Celtic would win the league. Marvin kept us going with his 'keep believing' mantra.*

One nice moment for me came when Alex McLeish came into the dressing room and said to me: 'Marvin, you are actually a god now at Ibrox.' It was special, particularly since I had been written off as a squad player by many when I first joined the club and here I was at the centre of one of Rangers' greatest successes.

After the match, the players headed back to Ibrox on the team bus, but I had a prior arrangement to attend the church service in Kirkcaldy that evening and I was picked up by Paster Joe Nwokoye. While the rest of the party headed westwards to Ibrox, I sat in a car headed towards Fife. It took ages for our car to get through the crowds of Rangers fans who surrounded the vehicle, banging on the windows and saying: 'You were right Marvin, we believe.' Others lay down in front of the car and said: 'Run over us. We'll be okay, because we believe.' They were rocking the car as we were engulfed with people. It was a fantastically delirious crowd.

Eventually, we got through the hordes and headed northwards over the Forth Road Bridge. When we arrived at the church, everyone was there for the normal service. Much of it was devoted to my experience of winning the title in the most unlikely of circumstances. I gave my testimony, thanking God for delivering this wonderful experience in Edinburgh. Again, I praised the Lord for fulfilling our dream of the championship. After the service ended and I had spoken with the congregation for some time, I drove down to Glasgow to meet up with the rest of the squad. They had gone back to Ibrox where, remarkably, a crowd of 40,000 awaited to greet them. As I drove back to the city, I reflected on how happy I was and kept asking myself: 'Has this really happened?' A few weeks earlier, I had been written off because of my injury, but here I was celebrating a win on one of the best days of my life. I should not even have been on the pitch, by all accounts, but here I was and a major part of it all.

While I was back in Kirkcaldy, the players enjoyed their celebrations inside our ground. After taking the applause of the crowds and proudly waving the trophy in ecstasy, they had gone inside the stadium. I gather the celebrations continued at Ibrox for some time before the players got changed to head out into the city to a nightclub called Tiger Tiger. When I arrived to join them late in the evening, it was one of the most emotional experiences of my life. As soon as I walked in, everyone stood up and applauded. I was wearing another T-shirt with a similar script to that I had worn on the field, this time celebrating our win.

It was a fantastic day and it will always go down as one of the greatest in Rangers' history. Every Light Blues fan has a story to tell about what they were doing, wherever they were in the world, on Helicopter Sunday. Generations upon generations of Rangers supporters will be told the story of that day and I am so proud to have been involved.

We never gave up that season. After 38 league games, we were separated from Celtic by a solitary point, but it was enough. That phrase 'keep believing' was iconic and even today the fans remind me of it and how poignant and appropriate it was on that fateful day in Edinburgh. Even now, years later, fans call out to me: 'Marv, keep believing.' Many fans I meet still want to talk about Helicopter Sunday. Hopefully, some of those who experienced those dramatic events will reflect on their faith and note that those iconic words of 'keep believing' were not an empty sentiment.

I look back on my whole Rangers career with a big smile on my face and great joy. Helicopter Sunday was one of the greatest days of my career. It was a day when I was also on a learning curve, understanding what it was all about to play for such a great club in such an historic match. I am so proud that I was able to play at Easter Road and give the supporters one of the most memorable days in the club's history. Reflecting on that day, I feel so honoured and thankful to God for giving me the chance to play for such a fantastic club as Rangers.

After the celebrations ended in Glasgow in the early hours, I returned to my home in Kirkcaldy and had a quiet reflection on where it had all started for me, back in Mount Lambert, Trinidad. I again thanked God for fulfilling my prayers. I could not have imagined how life would turn out for me and how the Lord had charted my course. Importantly, I think my team-mates and many of the fans appreciated my 'keep believing' message, although they never did come to my church afterwards as they had promised. Perhaps they would rue that when things did not go so well the next season, but on 22 May 2005 we were in the moment.

Reflecting on that day, Rangers essentially won the championship in two minutes. It showed to me that God can wait until the very last to fulfil your desire. It is not about believing for five or ten minutes, but you should continue to believe that things will work out eventually. Belief in God is not for lifting and laying. Though the path may be painful, you need to trust in God to the end. I still pinch myself and try to get my head round the events that day in Easter Road. How did it all happen? It was a miracle and I thank God for it. The words on my T-shirt resonated and are worth repeating here: 'The things that are impossible with men are possible with God.'

Perhaps there is a little lesson for us all in that.

Chapter Two

Hardship, but Happiness in San Juan

I WAS born on 22 December 1975 in the town of San Juan, close to Port of Spain, on the island paradise of Trinidad. It is more than 5,000 miles away from Scotland and a world away from my adopted homeland in many respects. A little bit of background on the island before I go on. Trinidad (the Spanish word for 'trinity') was discovered by Christopher Columbus in 1498 and it was he who named the island. He apparently considered the name apt, since his vista on his approach to the south of the island was the Southern Range of hills with its three peaks. It is also said that he wanted to honour the Holy Trinity.

The island is the larger of the two which form the single entity known as Trinidad and Tobago. They were combined as a single administration by the British in 1889 and, in 1962, gained independence, finally becoming a republic the year after I was born.

The period was a good one economically for Trinidad and Tobago. It had extensive oil reserves and when the price of oil went up, the country experienced something of a boom. Unlike most other Caribbean countries, it did not rely so much on tourism, so these should have been good times for the population of around 1.3m. Unemployment, which had previously been high, went down as opportunities for work opened up for many of the people.

With a good supply of work and a great climate, you may think of it as an island paradise. The images of the island landscape might seem heavenly, with beautiful green tree-clad hills and sun-drenched beaches fringing the coastline like white ribbons. Then there is the blue sky and the deep blue ocean.

For many of the islanders and visitors it was, indeed, blissful. However, life was not so idyllic for me through my early childhood.

My mother, Cynthia Albino, was only 16 when I was born. She was barely more than a child herself and did not have the maturity to bring up a baby. The consensus in the family was that she was just too young to shoulder the responsibility at that time. She liked to party and had a reputation for being a bit of a rebel, living life to the full. Despite her active social life, she was not in a good place as a young lady. She was also a Shango Baptist and they had cult-like practices that were completely at variance with the Christian beliefs I would later adopt.

I discuss the Shango Baptist religion later in the book (Chapter 11).

One night, after I had been left without care, my dad, Anthony Andrews, decided that it was better for my welfare if I lived elsewhere. He worked during the day and if my mum was not able to care for me, it was better for another member of the family to step in. I went to my auntie initially, but then the responsibility was placed upon my grandmother – my dad's mother. Her name was Isidora Rose Andrews, but we knew her by the name 'Tah'. She would have a huge influence in my life. My dad lived in the house with us, although it would be my gran who would rear me. Within a year, my mother had another child – my brother, Micah. She looked after Micah for a little while before he also joined me at my grandmother's house. While I knew all of my relatives on my dad's side of the family, I never knew my grandparents or anyone else from my mum's side.

My grandmother was the head of the household and had always been the family matriarch. We were raised strictly by her, but it was all done in our best interests, as her only focus was in watching out for us. There was not much money around at that time, with my dad providing the main source of income. He was a few years older than my mum and, unlike her, was living responsibly. He had a good job working at the wharf and provided enough money for our care. He also earned a bit of extra cash hustling on the streets, selling clothes and anything else he could get his hands on. Despite his endeavours, things remained tight financially, but my grandmother always made sure there was food on the table. The rest of the family contributed something to help support her and, after handling the daily costs, she still managed to put some money aside for savings.

Her house was very much the hub for the family and she tried to keep everyone together. When I initially went to live there with my dad, the only other person in the home, apart from my grandmother, was a younger auntie. She lived in a small room at the back of the house. However, other members of the family were always coming and going, sometimes staying for anything up to a few days. It is quite normal in the West Indies for extended families to live together and ours was very much that kind of an open house.

Even after Micah moved in to join me at my grandmother's house, he also spent a bit of time, on occasions, living with my mum, while I remained at home. I think that, as my dad's first-born, my gran gave me a bit more special attention. From my earliest years, she really took a shine to me, praying for me every night. She cared for my every need and everywhere she went, I was always by her side. She was preparing me for life, including how to look after myself at home. With her guidance, I would help out domestically with everything from ironing shirts to baking cakes. She even took me on my first flight in an aeroplane. Despite her care and being reared in a loving home, my upbringing was strict under her. However, no matter how comforted and protected I felt at her home, I was always conscious that my mum was out there. I have vivid memories of her standing outside my grandmother's house and shouting: 'Give me my son, give me my son.' I would only have been an infant at the time, but the images remain fresh in my mind. I did not really understand the whole situation because I was too young to really comprehend what was happening. There is no doubt that she really wanted me back, but I am not sure that she could have raised me in the same environment I had at my gran's. Regardless of her undoubted anguish at times, the family felt that it was best for me to stay with my grandmother, because of my mum's troubles.

Despite wanting me back, my mum never came to our home apart from those few incidences of shouting outside the house. I did not get a chance to see her regularly until much later when I went to high school and moved nearer to her, in the area of Petit Bourg, San Juan. I would often meet her in the street, which gave us the chance to sit down and chat. By then, I think she realised that moving in with my grandmother had been the best thing for me. Over the years, her life has moved on and now I have nine siblings in total – six sisters and three brothers, mostly all from different fathers. Whenever I go back to Trinidad, I try to catch up with most of them from time to time. As the oldest and most successful, some of them will occasionally call me for advice. However, of all my siblings, I am naturally closest to Micah, with whom I shared our father and my early life.

Looking back, I realise it must have been difficult for my mum in those years and, despite all the problems she endured, the family did not abandon her. I understand that early on they had tried to put her on the right path, but to no avail. Eventually she responded to our orchestrations to help her rehabilitation and now she is in a much better place. She is obviously an older and more mature woman now and we are probably closer than we have ever been. She did lots of crazy stuff in her life, but I am not in the least resentful. In fact, I think she is brilliant and I am so pleased to have her as my mum. I speak with her every few days and she has now settled into a nice comfortable life. I speak with my dad every other day too and he has been an important part of my life.

Looking back, I can see that living with my grandmother was the making of me. She was highly principled and tried to ensure that my brother and I learned how to live the right way. This came from her great inner strength and deep faith in God. This is fundamentally where the strength of my own faith originated. She encouraged me to pray every day, as I still do. I prayed first thing in the morning with thanks for the breath of life that God had given me and last thing at night for getting me safely through the day with a new one to look forward to. Her religious guidance was fundamental to how she led her life and she naturally conveyed that to me.

Besides her religious principles, my grandmother led me on the path to be a good person. As kids, she instilled in us a respect for our elders and educated us in politeness, ensuring we said 'good morning' and 'good day' to people in a kindly way. She also taught me that I should treat people properly in my dealings with them. It was a good grounding in decency and in my everyday life I still try to follow all of the principles she taught us.

That is not to say that I am perfect. I am not and I have never claimed to be. Like everyone else, I have made mistakes. But one aspect of life that I have held strongly is a respect for people and their property. You must work hard to earn money to survive and I believe that honest endeavour deserves reward. If hard work brings material things, then anyone can quite rightly be proud of the fruits of their labour. To be able to say 'this is mine and I worked for it' is laudable. Conversely, I can never understand those who revel in their ill-gotten gains. It is abhorrent that some make their way through life by stealing or earn money through activities that can only be considered evil. I would never steal and, from an early age, I was reared to realise it is wrong. This is just one of life's rules that I picked up as a child.

Both Micah and I had to abide by my grandmother's strict rules while living in her home and I am certain that

I would not be the man I am now without that guidance. Her belief was that if children were trained to follow the right path at an early age, they would continue on that road. Now, she has children and grandchildren all over the world who continue to live as she taught them. I owe her a huge debt of gratitude for the guiding light she provided in keeping my life on the right track from my early years. Since she led a good Christian life, my grandmother wanted us to let Christ into our hearts. Besides our daily prayers, she encouraged us to go to church, as she did. She believed that this would place my brother and I into the presence of God.

As I said earlier, my mother was a Shango Baptist, which was a quasi-religious group that had quite fundamental beliefs. She became increasingly drawn in by them. In many ways, they are like a cult with quite radical ways. Most of my family were Shango Baptists and my grandmother had been too, but she had pulled away to adopt more mainstream Christian beliefs.

Catholicism was the largest Christian faith in Trinidad at the time and Mount Lambert Roman Catholic Church was within walking distance of our home. All of our family were Baptists, but because of the proximity of the church to her home, my gran went there. It was natural that she would also introduce us to that church and, besides being convenient, it seemed suited and welcoming to children. Their Sunday school was the best and eventually I took first communion at the church, becoming confirmed as a Roman Catholic. That became the foundation for my faith.

Next door to the church was Mount Lambert Primary School, the first school I attended, as a five-year-old in 1980. I have nothing but good memories of the school, having fun with the other kids and playing 'scooch'. This is a game we used to play with a tennis ball with all the fur stripped from it. If we were in the possession of the ball, we would try to hit one of our friends with it and then it would be their turn to do likewise. You never liked being hit on your back, though, because it would sting when the ball was wet. I guess it is similar to the game dodgeball, which many British kids would have been more familiar with. I had a great teacher – from memory, her name was Miss Peruza – and she helped me a lot. I always enjoyed school but, as a young kid, it was much more fun playing outside.

I was at the school for only a year or so when the first big tragedy in my life struck. My grandmother was suffering from breast cancer and sadly died. Her passing was traumatic for me and, indeed, all my relatives. She had been such a big part of all our lives – our rock.

As I look back on my time with her, I realise how well she raised me in those formative years. I am comforted to think that she would have been so happy to learn how my life has turned out. My aunties have so often told me how much she loved me, saying that she would have been over the moon to see how my life evolved. I must give her a lot of the credit for that. When she passed, I discovered that she had left 15,000 Trinidad and Tobago dollars (about £3,000 at that time), accumulated through her meticulous saving with the Western Union Bank, in an account for me. It was humbling that she had set aside some money for me each year, especially since we were not a rich household. It gives some measure of the love she had for me.

After her death, I stopped going to church. I had actually wanted to be an altar boy but, as time went on, I saw that this particular church was not all that I expected and I witnessed some things that disturbed me. I was also disaffected by that church's religious practices and it no longer represented my ideals. By then, my own personal beliefs had evolved, because faith comes from within. I affiliated with the Baptists, who have strong beliefs but worship God in a different way. As I say, my grandmother's beliefs, too, were more aligned to that Baptist church, but the proximity of the Catholic church brought it into her life and then mine. At this time, I would pray morning and night as my grandmother had taught me, but I did not read the scriptures. Religion did not feature in my life as strongly as it does now. It was only when I came to Scotland that it would become a major part of my life, as I shall explain later.

I was maturing and about to enter another phase in my life. After my gran died, I stayed at the house for three and a half years, until the family sold it off. Then, my brother, dad and I had to find somewhere else to live. We moved in with my grandfather, who lived a short distance away at Irving Street in a little community known as Petit Bourg in the north of San Juan. Moving to that area gave me more freedom to get out to play, but I was also conscientious about doing well with my schoolwork. I knew education could give me the basis for a good future. The system in Trinidad and Tobago was similar to that in Scotland. When I was 11 and at the end of my primary school years, I sat what was called the common entrance examination. This was like the old Scottish 11-plus examination. There was huge pressure on everyone to pass this exam, as it gave children a chance to direct their education to the school they wanted. If you failed, you stayed at primary school, regardless of age. I buckled down and worked hard to prepare for my examinations. I was delighted when I passed, successfully earning entry to Mount Hope Junior Secondary School.

While school was great, I could not wait to get outside to play games. With so many great and famous cricketers emerging from Trinidad and Tobago, it was natural that we played the game, generally in the street and using a tennis ball. However, I gave up any ideas of playing organised cricket matches after seeing how dangerous it could be with the hard leather cricket ball. In one game in which I played when I was younger, the wicketkeeper took a fast delivery of the ball full in the face. There was blood everywhere and I decided there and then it was not the game for me. It is quite ironic really because, over the years playing football, I have taken knocks and gashes to my face, with blood frequently pouring down on to my shirt. In my football career, I have probably suffered more cuts and grazes than the average cricketer.

Although cricket was popular, every kid played football and the game quickly got a grip on me. We would play anywhere there was enough space; the street or any open ground where goals either existed or could be created. At that time, I was smaller than most of the guys on the block, so I tended to get knocked over easily, but I just picked myself up and got on with it. That was the way of things. You had to look after yourself, which I quickly learned.

People in the UK would probably find it hard to believe that many of us did not have any footwear when we played the game as kids. Quite simply, when I was young, there was a period when my dad could not afford to buy me trainers or boots. So, like many of my friends, I did not think anything of playing without them. Playing on rough ground really hardened up the soles of my feet. We often played five-a-side in an old quarry with sharp gravel and rubble underfoot, so if the soles of our feet were not hard, it would leave us in a mess. Even so, it was tough and I lost many a toenail or stubbed my feet on the hard ground. I even resorted to trying flip-flops to make it a bit easier on my soles, but they kept falling off when I was running, so they were of no real use. If I burst a toe,

I just wrapped it up with cloth and got on with the game. Injuries like that were commonplace, but my friends and I just had to brush it all aside. We did not care, because we just loved the sport.

Eventually, when my dad was working at the docks as an engineer, he was earning good wages and was able to buy me a pair of new adidas trainers (size eight and a half). In fact, I got a new pair every school term, as I was going through them at that rate. It was hardly surprising because I wore them all the time, playing every day. If it was not football, then we would play basketball or cricket (with a tennis ball, of course!). I was never in the house and looked for every chance of getting outside to join my pals playing whatever game took our fancy. Most of the time, it was football.

Having been playing mostly in the street and reaching a decent level, the school offered me the chance to play in their football team – the first properly organised game I would play. That was a bit later than boys in Britain and even some in Trinidad and Tobago. Russell Latapy, for example, who would also eventually play for Rangers, had started playing at a much younger age. He was even playing representative football for the Under-10s and then later for the Under-14s, so I was a bit late to the party.

At the school, I was encouraged to take the game more seriously than I had done in the street. It became more structured, with everyone allocated positions. The school coach saw me more as a defender because of my heading ability. He had noted that I would think nothing of returning a kick from the keeper with a header that could carry 40 or 50 yards. People would ask if it hurt, but it didn't. It was just something that came naturally to me but, at that time, I did not have any inclination to play in defence. I saw myself as a striker or a winger. Even though my heading ability was a big asset in defence, I still fancied getting in on the goals. I loved scoring goals and I used to go up into the opposition box for set pieces, getting more than my fair share with my head.

It was around this time that I got my nickname in Trinidad. On the playing field they called me 'Dog' after seeing me frantically running all over the field in one game. One guy called out, 'You're acting like a dog,' and the name just stuck from then on. Many felt it was even more appropriate when I got older, as they thought I was like a Rottweiler! Back home in Trinidad and Tobago, I am still known as 'Dog', even among the media guys.

It was while living in Petit Bourg that I began to really enjoy my newfound freedom. Away from school, I spent most of my time out on the street playing football with my friends. In truth, I was never really at home. It was around then that I really learned a lot more about the skills of the game, through my cousin, Shawn David. He was two or three years older than me and played for Malick Senior Comprehensive, which had a great team. They won nine zonal and national league titles, as well as the North Zone InterCol competition. Many players who had served Malick went on to play in the national team. Shawn was the top man in the Malick team, very talented, and I used to go and watch him play. He saw my interest in the game and provided a lot of encouragement, helping me develop my own ability. Despite his skill, Shawn never really developed to his full potential as a footballer, but he was a great inspiration for me in those early years.

My dad had been a decent footballer too and played amateur football as a pretty rugged defender, but he had no desire to become a professional. When he played, it was only a sport, not a profession. It was not until some time later that football was considered a potential way of earning a living. Sadly, not long after we moved in with my grandfather, he also died. There was a further major change in my life when my dad lost his job and was finding work hard to come by. The luxury of new trainers that I had once enjoyed every school term ended. Our financial difficulties coincided with the collapse of the island's economy in the late 1980s and unemployment rose to more than 20 per cent. Things became tough for all of us and I experienced hard times. My dad had always had a good work ethic and when he lost his job at the docks, he just hustled more on the streets. However, it was tough and, like many others, he would discover that the economic crash led to the usual sources of income running dry.

Poverty impacted every aspect of our life. Our daily food, which was spread throughout the family, was limited to sausage, bread and Kool-Aid, a drink sold in powdered form as a concentrate and mixed with water to provide a flavoured drink. It was a cheap alternative to bottled juices. One of the benefits of living in a tropical climate is that fruit trees are plentiful and I used these to supplement my meagre rations.

The problem was that many of these trees were in people's gardens, so I had to sneak in and gather fruit which was lying around the ground. I gathered mangoes, oranges, pears and sugar cane, which all helped to supplement my diet. These were the only things I have ever 'stolen', but it was simply because we were so hungry. I also got coconuts. I could never climb palm trees, but I had a friend who was good at getting up there. He would cut the coconuts loose and I would be the 'catcher'.

There were no new clothes and my wardrobe was barren. I had one pair of jeans, one T-shirt and one pair of trainers, although I was rapidly growing out of all of them. It seemed that there were no real prospects for my dad in Trinidad, so he went to New York in 1990 to see if he could make a better life for us there. However, he didn't find it much easier in the 'Big Apple' and never managed to send for us to join him there. He did, though, keep money flowing back to Trinidad to help support my brother and I.

I was 14 when my dad went away and we obviously could not live alone in Trinidad. The rest of my aunts and uncles disliked my dad, so my auntie, Claudette Roberts, stepped forward to take responsibility for us. She was the only one who showed any interest in us. Most treated us with disdain, saying that all we could do was kick a football around and that we would never make anything of our lives. That attitude made me doubly determined to become a success.

At that time, Claudette was coming around to the house to look after us, but she was going through her own problems. Although she still lived with her partner at her own house, which was situated nearby at Santa Cruz, she was in the process of separating. It was not an ideal situation, especially when we discovered that my grandfather had left the house to one of my uncles in his will. The uncle did not get on with my dad, so he asked us to leave and we had to look for somewhere else to live. By then, Claudette had separated and bought a new house. We moved in with her and when she decided to renovate it, we helped her. Her house was made of timber and boards, but she decided to refurbish it, rebuilding it with brick. Because of its location on a hilltop and the absence of an access road a vehicle could negotiate, I carried the bricks, cement, sand and timber up the hill. That helped build me up physically.

Claudette was a bit of a rebel and very strict with us, which occasionally led to some dissent. My brother and I were typical teenagers and we sometimes gave her a hard time, but we never disrespected her. Ultimately, it was her house and although she threatened to lock us out sometimes, it was never a serious threat. She always relented and one of my memories is that she was always there for us.

Around this time, I had become old enough to go to the fourth form at San Juan Senior Comprehensive School. Life at that school was really the making of me in football. When I moved there, I could have joined the football team at the start, but I was less inclined to do so because I was a shy boy. People might find that strange, knowing that I am first to the microphone for anyone who wants a rendition of 'Four Lads Had a Dream!'

Rather than putting myself forward as a potential player, I used to go and watch the school team play. I was eager to join them but I lacked confidence, worrying that I might not be good enough. They were older players and I thought they would be much better and tougher opponents than I had been used to facing. That might be hard to believe, given the physicality I developed later in my career, but I was timid and scared at that time. Recognising my enthusiasm for the game, my schoolmates kept asking me to play and, in my final year, I relented, saying I would give it a try. So, the next time the school called for boys to represent it at football, I put my name forward, eventually being selected for the team. Looking back, it was probably the best decision I made at that time.

The team coach, Miguel (Mikey) Hackett, had been a seasoned defender who had made the international side.

He had great footballing credentials and I was eager to learn from him. As a defender, he knew my position well and his advice proved invaluable in teaching me how to defend properly. I was good in the air, but he helped me improve at set pieces, attacking the ball at corners and free kicks. Another aspect of my game he worked on was in how to read the game. It was all about seeing where the danger would come from and understanding how a game was playing out. I learned a lot from him.

Miguel, who was an ex-soldier, coached us all well, but his abilities went beyond the action on the playing field. He knew how to handle the kids and that played such an important role in developing the youngsters socially. He showed them how football could change their outlook in the community. The school had a reputation as being violent and when I first went there, we were screened for knives and other weapons. It would be easy for many of the youngsters to wander down the wrong track, but Miguel knew that if he could develop their interest in football, it would help steer some of them in the right direction. Football gave them a focus and if they wanted to play for the school, they would have to leave any notions of violence and crime behind them. It helped them see a way that they could do something positive in their lives.

Many of the kids benefitted from his advice, but sadly others would go down a path that could lead them to ruin. They included some of my friends, who carried knives and even guns. I had the sense to know that I should not allow weapons to enter my life. It was something that never interested me and I was never drawn to even touch any kind of weapon, let alone carry one. Violence and crime were not so far away in parts of the community, but I was fortunate that I had been reared to know the path that I had to follow. I was maturing, and as you get older, you get wiser. Besides, I was fortunate that away from school, I did not live in a particularly tough area. There was hardly any violent crime where I lived, so I was not exposed to it as much as others, who most certainly were. The people who lived in our part of the community had their own social problems, but violence was not generally one of them.

Miguel's coaching and guidance helped me tie down a place in the team and I became one of his key players. The work I had put in on my heading ability helped me get on the scoresheet for the team, scoring five goals from corners. We started to see some real rewards in our performances and our team reached two cup semi-finals and finished third in the league.

By then, all I could think about was football. In fact, I was enjoying the game so much that I decided to repeat the year at school. That allowed me to stay with the team and continue playing in an atmosphere I loved. It was a fantastic time for me.

I had done well at San Juan and when I left at 16, I was pleased to learn that I had come to the attention of the international selectors. I was chosen to play for my country at Under-18 level. The authorities had pulled together 100 of the best players from around the schools with a view to whittling them down to just 18. I was delighted to make that contingent and went on to make the squad for the CONCACAF qualifying matches for the Under-20 World Cup. We didn't make it through, but I played well and it was great knowing that I was on the radar of the selectors.

Throughout the hardships we endured, with poverty and then the departure of my dad to the USA, football had always provided some respite for me. Despite doing well, however, I never really saw it as a profession. It was just a game to be played and enjoyed. Aside from my own experiences in football, I was keenly interested in how the international team was doing. In 1992, when I left school, the interest in the national side had begun to grow again. Whenever there were big international matches, the interest throughout Trinidad and Tobago was massive. The crowds in the stadia were big and for those who could not be there, there was decent TV coverage. For the big matches, those without a TV would gather outside television shops to peer at the screens in the window. Playing at a higher level, albeit in school football, had enhanced my love for the game. Dreams of going further were stirred, but could I imagine that I might eventually be selected for my country? It seemed so far away, or maybe not so after my appearance for the Under-18 side. My more immediate priority was getting a job now that school had ended. Little did I know that this would provide a pathway to my passion – football.

Chapter Three

The Path to a Career in Football

SCOTLAND'S ROLE in the development of football goes back to the earliest days, but some might wonder when the interest in the game in Trinidad and Tobago emerged. I was surprised to discover recently that there were Scottish roots to its emergence in my country. Interestingly, considering that I would go on to play for Rangers, who are based in Glasgow, football was introduced by a man from the city, named Thomas Boyd. He had arrived on the island in the 1890s as a teenager, one of many Scots who came to help manage trade and the sugar estates.

Historical context – *The arrival of people from the UK, and notably Scotland, at that time was not universally accepted. The general feeling amongst the islanders was highlighted in the* Trinidad News *and* San Fernando Gazette *of 6 June 1893. It reported that there was growing corruption among the local youths, which they attributed to the arrival of 'strangers from the United*

Kingdom'. They noted that the local youths had been subject to 'growing corruption by frequentation of places of evil, gambling halls, dignity balls etc'.

The newspaper continued: 'It would be knocking our heads against a stone wall to find fault with Scotsmen who now have the dry goods trade and the management of sugar estates mostly in their hands because they send their poor relatives or friends from Scotland to fill situations of emoluments under them. We believe our creole youth to be brighter than the young strangers who are imported to occupy posts which, of right, should be theirs and with the knowledge they have of people, their ways, their language, and their wants, they would certainly be more useful. But it is a fact that in the majority of cases, they are distanced by strangers and facts are stubborn things.'

Thomas Boyd may well have been that kind of 'stranger' who arrived on the island, but if some of his compatriots could be a disruptive influence to the youth of Trinidad, he would go on to show that he could contribute well to the local society. He loved football and had apparently dreamed of playing for Scotland, but the island did not offer any opportunity to play, let alone get to the standard of the national side. Boyd had settled in Port of Spain and looked around for a football field, but there was none. Searching for a location where the game could be played, he was attracted to 'the Savannah', a huge flat-lying park which was used for grazing cattle in the centre of the city. In fact, every park is called the savannah in Trinidad nowadays, but then it was a specific area that was well known to the locals.

While he thought that the Savannah would be ideal for playing football, he could not find a single football in the colony. He sent out a plea to his family back home in Scotland and they posted a ball out to him along with two bladders and an inflator. Initially he was uncertain how many people would be interested in playing, but quickly learned there would be no shortage of enthusiasts for a game.

In fact, after Boyd had circulated the expat community, he was delighted to find that 30 turned up for that first game, with jackets and caps thrown down as goalposts. It was the 'winter game' back in Scotland, but the heat and humidity of the Trinidad climate eventually culled the number of enthusiasts, leaving them with 12 who were keen as mustard. It became something of a social afternoon for the 'players' as they exchanged news of back home. Eventually they formed themselves into a club, attracting new members with every group that came out to Trinidad.

Half of the time was spent on exchanging news of developments back 'home'. They eventually played matches against the local Queens Park Cricket Club and, on Boyd's initiative, the British Rovers Club was formed. This club was the pioneer club for the football in the colony.

How ironic that I would learn this game introduced by a Scotsman in my country, then eventually play for the biggest club in Scotland. Not only that, but when Boyd's club, the British Rovers, faded a few years after formation, he helped found the Clydesdale Cricket Club in 1897, which, although primarily a cricket club, also had a football section. I know that before Rangers settled at Ibrox, the club had played at Kinning Park on the former field of the Glasgow version of the Clydesdale Cricket Club. The two clubs carried the same name but were probably unrelated.

As the game grew in popularity and more clubs were created, a football association was formed in 1908. It was called the Trinidad Amateur Football Association (TAFA), with Boyd as its first president. The association had six football clubs and 194 registered players in that inaugural 1908/09 season. The early clubs were formed loosely around ethnic or church groups. Few, if any, indigenous Trinidadians were included in the teams. However, by 1909, a team known as Majestic, which was established by and made up of locals, joined the league. Within three years, TAFA had gained affiliation to the Football Association in England and the game was thriving on the island. The popularity of the game increased rapidly from then.

Of course, while football became extremely popular in Trinidad and Tobago, cricket was the number one sport. Over the years, it had produced some real national heroes including Brian Lara, Sonny Ramadhin and Baron Learie Constantine. Besides being a test cricketer of the highest level, the Baron became a senior politician and was influential in the passing of the 1965 Race Relations Act in Britain. However, Trinidad and Tobago's obsession with football was growing and there was huge public interest in 1973 when the country played in the World Cup qualifying matches for the 1974 finals in West Germany. Trinidad and Tobago were in a six-nation qualifying tournament played in Port-au-Prince, Haiti, which also featured the hosts, Mexico, Honduras, Guatemala and Netherlands Antilles. Only the top team would go through. Trinidad and Tobago eventually lost out in controversial fashion.

I had not even been born at that point, but I learned about the circumstances, which were hugely unfair. When Trinidad and Tobago faced Haiti, the hosts won 2-1 with a goal scored with just two minutes remaining of a match in which Trinidad and Tobago had four goals disallowed them for some obscure infringement. The defeat proved decisive as Haiti went on to qualify, finishing two points ahead of our team and Mexico. Strangely, our national association did not protest, but the Mexicans did, albeit too late. The result stood, although the referee, who came from El Salvador, and a Canadian linesmen were subsequently banned indefinitely. We lost out in our quest for a place in West Germany and it would be another 15 years before we got a decent chance again.

By then, the experience in the match against Haiti all those years ago had reinforced the resolve of the nation. Our next realistic chance came in 1989 when we only needed a draw against the USA in the Hasely Crawford Stadium in our capital city Port of Spain to make it to Italia 90. I was just 14 at the time. The capacity of the ground was 30,000, but there were reportedly 50,000 there, with the rest of the population of the islands watching it on television. I sat glued to the television at my grandfather's house, wearing a red T-shirt; like just about everyone, I was sporting the team's colours for the match. I would say it was then that I developed a real enthusiasm for the game and a desire to play for my country.

The national team that year was probably the greatest in our history and everyone was behind them for the game. They were called the 'Strike Squad'. They carried all the hopes and expectations of the country on their shoulders. It was an enormous responsibility, but everyone believed we would get the result we needed to qualify for a World Cup for the first time.

After half an hour, American midfielder Paul Caligiuri drifted past one of our players and hit a shot which flew high in the air but, to the horror of everyone, dropped into the corner of the net. It was a poor goal to concede and our keeper claimed he had been blinded by the sunshine. Many blamed him for the error. Despite pushing on and desperately trying to get the vital equaliser, there was no more scoring and the game ended in a 1-0 defeat. We had fallen at the last hurdle.The country was devastated that another chance to qualify had gone. There was so much pain and sadness at that defeat and, football-wise, the country plunged into a deep and downward spiral. Interest in the game dipped after that, with negativity taking over and most people believing we would never qualify for a World Cup. If we could not do it with that great team, how could we ever manage to take that final step?

The general feeling was of despair and disillusionment, especially among the adults.

However, although the disappointment was huge, it did not quell the enthusiasm of a lot of the youngsters. Every young player dreamed of playing for the national side. I was no different. As I progressed in football, I began to feel that it was something that might just be attainable for me, but it still seemed just a dream. I knew that some youngsters were making progress in the game, but they were in structured programmes that introduced them to the national set-up quite early on. Competitions were introduced among the Under-12s, Under-14s, Under-16s and Under-18s. Players such as Russell Latapy and Dwight Yorke came through that route and Dwight played in the World Youth Championships. They were among some of the many great players who emerged from the system before going on to play with top teams in Europe. I, though, was not involved in any structured development programme and earning money from the game seemed a million miles away for me. I never really thought I would follow the likes of Yorke and Latapy into the professional game.

When I left school in 1992, I knew I would have to earn money and get a 'real' job. I was not afraid of hard work and I started off by selling fruits and vegetables in the marketplace, earning a dollar here and a dollar there. I did odd jobs like carrying bags and running errands for people, such as buying drink or marijuana for the old men on the street corners. Marijuana, like all narcotic drugs, was illegal in Trinidad and Tobago, but there were still millions of plants in the forested areas. The police instigated a programme known as 'Weedeater' to try to eradicate the plant, but that caused protests from the farmers who were growing it. Despite these efforts, it was still rife and popular among the population, especially the older folks.

There was nothing unusual about young kids running to get marijuana for their elders and I guess it was not much different from the UK where kids would run for cigarettes for their parents. Both my parents smoked marijuana occasionally, but I never had any inclination to do so. I saw the evils of drugs and the destruction they could leave behind. It is something that stuck with me and left me with a determination in later years to do something to help youngsters addicted to drugs and drink.

None of these odd jobs were particularly satisfying, but at least they were better than when I was asked to dig toilet holes – latrines and sewer holes. It was not the most glamorous of jobs, but at least it generated some money. Looking back at these days, I was living my life as what they called a 'hustler' – earning money through jobs I could pick up on the streets, as my dad had done – and I had no steady employment. All the time, I was progressing in football and it was through this that I managed to get my first 'proper' job, at 17.

I had joined a team called Motown FC, who were sponsored by an electrical firm that was involved in the construction industry. Through the team's connections, the opportunity came to work on building sites as a general labourer, carrying mortar and toting lumber. It was hard physical work, but after doing a stint carrying bricks, cement and other construction materials uphill for my aunt's house, it was manageable. All that lifting and carrying really built me up and improved my general fitness, adding strength as well as stamina. When I got that first cheque of around £150 at the end of the week, I felt so good that I was now making a life for myself, earning my own money. I had a job and was playing good football with a decent team. What more could I ask for?

Bob Malcolm (Former Team-mate at Rangers FC) – *When Marvin joined us at Rangers and took off his shirt in the dressing room, we noticed how chiselled his body was with great abdominal muscles, even though* *we would never see him in the gym. He told us that his work back in Trinidad on the building sites and in the Carib Brewery carrying boxes of beer, had helped him build up good body strength and shape.*

After playing for the national Under-18 team and Motown FC, my name was becoming better known through football and was appearing in the newspapers. Sometimes I even featured on television, which was a nice but strange experience. Then, after about a year with Motown FC, one of my mates suggested I join him at another semi-professional team, Carib FC.

Football in Trinidad was regionalised and Carib FC were in the East Zone. There would be a job opportunity as part of their set-up, too. The club were formed under the company that produced the country's lager – Carib Brewery – and that is where I would next work. Not only that, but I would eventually discover that it was this move that would eventually change the direction of my life.

I had an interview with the general manager at the brewery, Tim Nafziger. He was an American who had come to Trinidad from a farming background in 1973. I was to find that he was a man who was popular with just about everyone. He loved sport and, in particular, football and was hugely supportive of the Carib FC football team during his time there. He was also supportive of the country's football federation and had built up some good contacts in the game.

It was through these connections that he helped Dwight Yorke on the path to a great career. Dwight played for a number of top English sides including Aston Villa, Blackburn Rovers, Birmingham City and Sunderland, but when he joined Manchester United and won some major honours, his name really came to prominence. He also played a number of times for Trinidad and Tobago. Dwight was considered to be one of Mr Nafziger's first 'discoveries' and he went on to look after him, acting as his agent.

As had been the case with FC Motown, where a job came along with a place in the team, I would not need to worry about work. Mr Nafziger had it all planned out for me. I would be employed by the brewery when I wasn't playing football. At first, he put me into the merchandising office and I also cleaned the building, going around the whole plant and offices. That might not sound very glamorous, but I loved it because it brought me into contact with so many of the workers. I built good relationships with them, widening my circle of friends. My daily routine began with an early start, but I settled into it very easily. I would get up at 3.30am, say my prayers and start work by 4.30am. Within four hours, I would have the whole place cleaned for the staff coming in at 8am. It left plenty of time for training and working on aspects of my game, because football was never far away from my daily schedule.

On the field, the team were doing superbly and I was playing well. We went on to win the league and I was really enjoying the football. When I had settled into it all, I got a change of role in the factory, joining the production line. That's where most of the football team worked and where more money was to be made. Colin Murray was the PR man for Carib and the football team manager. He went on to become heavily involved in sports throughout the country and helped many through the sponsorship the company offered. He was of enormous help to me during my time at the brewery, working things so that I got shifts on the line that fitted in better with the demands of the team.

When I started working on the production line, I started to drink lager – the company's product. It could be oppressively hot inside the factory and occasionally we would reach over for a bottle of this lovely cool lager. The managers knew it was happening and if they had caught us, we could have been sacked, but we needed to quench our thirst in the heat. I do not know how many bottles I drank in a day, but it just added to the whole carefree life I followed back then. I could quite happily have remained at Carib forever, continuing to play football locally with no motivation to go anywhere else. Life was so enjoyable at the brewery and, as well as working hard, I was training hard for the team.

The recognition of playing for the national Under-18 team was wonderful, but I was desperate to play a full international. What had seemed a dream just a short time before was increasingly shaping up to be as a distinct possibility. Seven years earlier, I had watched on TV as the national side played a vital World Cup qualifying match. Now, I could sense that the opportunity to play in such a match was just a short step away. I was being selected more regularly for representative teams at different age levels. After I had played for the national Under-20 squad, I went on to play for a select international team made up mainly of players from the Under-18, Under-20 and Under-23 teams. We travelled to Colombia for a friendly and lost 3-0 in what was my first real taste of representative football for Trinidad and Tobago.

The coach for the national side was a Serbian, Zoran Vraneš. His footballing credentials were impressive, both as a player and in coaching. He had played with both Red Star Belgrade and Partizan Belgrade before making a successful move into management. He had arrived in Trinidad and Tobago in 1994 and had started to make an impact on the national side. He was excellent and, more importantly, he really believed in me. I had met him a few times in the age group international games, so he knew all about me. He had given me that first chance at senior representative football in that match against Colombia. I was just 20 years old and, although we had lost, I settled well into the game, playing well enough to be in the squad for the World Cup qualifiers.

The 1998 World Cup finals would be played in France and there would be three spots available to CONCACAF, with 30 teams from North and South America, and the Caribbean competing for them. I did not feature in the early stages of the qualifying competition, including the second round when we beat the Dominican Republic home and away. That took us into the third round, which was a league section and included the USA, Costa Rica, Guatemala and ourselves. Each of the teams would play against each other home and away.

We performed poorly in the first three matches, losing to Costa Rica, drawing with Guatemala and then going down 2-0 away to the United States. One point from these first three games in the section was poor and the defeats were down mostly to some bad defensive errors. I had not featured in any of the games, but I came into the reckoning for the next match, which was the return against the United States. It came just two weeks after our away defeat by them and would be played at our home ground in Port of Spain on 24 November 1996.

When the team was announced, I was only on the bench, but I did get a chance to come on for Anthony Rougier at the start of the second half. It was my first full international cap and was in a competitive game. By the time I came on, we were already a goal down after a dreadful defensive mix-up. We did not lose any more goals after I took to the field, but we could not get an equaliser and went on to lose 1-0. The result was a huge disappointment, but I was delighted that I had finally made the international side, especially in a World Cup qualifier.

I then played in further qualifiers against Guatemala, again coming on as substitute, and Costa Rica when I made my first full debut just before my 21st birthday. We narrowly lost both, which completed a poor campaign for us, but I was now in the international team – a dream fulfilled.

Things were looking good for me in life at this time. I was enjoying work and making good money, allowing me to save a bit and help my aunt too. No longer was I relying on others. I was becoming a man. I had no ambition to do any more. Working and playing football at Carib Brewery was satisfying. The standard of the team was high, despite them being part-time, and, although the guys enjoyed life and had a drink or two, we were hard to beat. Indeed, on the football field, things could not have been better. The Carib team were one of the best in the country and, of course, to have been capped by Trinidad and Tobago, playing in World Cup qualifiers, had been special.

I was content with life at Carib, but I would find that things were about to change radically and that my life would shift in another direction. It all began when I was presented with an opportunity that could have lured me away from Carib FC. I was approached by a club called Joe Public. They were owned by Jack Warner, who became vice-president of FIFA. He seemed to have his finger in every footballing pie around the Caribbean and was influential in not only football in the region, but also on the world stage. He eventually became implicated in numerous corruption scandals and was banned from football by FIFA in 2015. I was to later discover that he also had an involvement in my move to Scotland, but more on that later.

The Joe Public club had been formed when Warner tried to address the disappointment of the failed World Cup quest by setting up a professional league in 1996. His hope was that it would help produce more homegrown players who could compete internationally. The club paid their players higher wages than I could get at Carib FC. Although it would have been a good move for me financially to join Joe Public, I was settled at the brewery and declined their approach. However, Warner had not gone away. Seven months or so after I had made my international debut, I was stunned by a turn of events that would change my life forever. It was another footballing opportunity and while I had been in a position to decline the approach from Joe Public, that option would not be open to me this time. On this occasion, I would have to leave Carib FC because the whole affair was seemingly being orchestrated by them. It was late summer 1997 when Mr Nafziger called me into his office and said: 'I want you out of here. I'm sending you to Scotland. You have talent that is wasted here and you could do more with it by going away to play in a bigger league.'

It seemed harsh and uncompromising, but Mr Nafziger's words were not motivated by any desire he had to get me out of the team. He obviously saw better things for me in football than playing for Carib FC. It was the kind of situation that likely motivated his orchestration of Dwight Yorke's move to England. He told me that it was an opportunity to play in a good professional league in the UK, in Scotland to be precise. I did not know anything of the country or that it was even part of the UK until he told me. Neither did I know anything about the football or the teams that played there. I had seen English and Italian football on television, but not the game in Scotland. I could not even have told you the name of any clubs in the country.

Because I had a good relationship with Mr Nafziger and he had always been good with me at Carib, I trusted his judgement. If this was going to be a great chance for me, I had to embrace it, but the whole situation was dropped on me entirely without warning. When I went back home and told my family and friends, the few of those who knew anything about Scotland said: 'It's very cold – it snows there, Marvin!'

I was happily working at Carib and now I suddenly faced a trip to an alien land. I admit that I was not happy about the prospect at first, but Mr Nafziger told me I was not making the best of the talent that God had given me. He said that I should go out and show the world what I could do. Despite my reservations, I realised that he was right and that it was a chance to play professionally. There was no prospect for real progress in the game if I remained in Trinidad. In a sense, I had been playing purely for fun, but the time had been reached when I could be truly professional. It all depended on me being attractive to teams in Scotland, of course, but I was up for the challenge. It was now up to me to show those who would meet me in Scotland, whoever they were, that I could play and do a job for them. I was ready to seize the opportunity.

I have often wondered why my faith would take me to Scotland. Was it all part of a greater plan that God had for me? I would soon find out that the warnings about the cold were true, but I would also later learn that Scotland provided a route for players from the Caribbean to get into the game professionally and perhaps move on to greater things. Finances were tight for most clubs in Scotland, but they had discovered that they could attract seasoned international players from the Caribbean for modest costs, then build them into decent assets. Most teams could not afford the best players from their own leagues and most others in Europe, but the Caribbean, and particularly Trinidad and Tobago, was a fertile market for players.

Besides being good business for the Scottish clubs, a move into the game there gave the best talent that the Caribbean could muster a chance to play against better players. The standard was high and it is only by playing at that level that players could progress. Of course, nothing was certain at that time, because I would have to show clubs that I could perform and be of value to them. I did not know which clubs I would be introduced to or the money that could be on offer. It truly was a step into the dark, with my future seemingly in the hands of others. Where would I live, how would I fit in, what would the people be like, was this the right country for me? These were just some of the questions that revolved in my mind, all the time having faith that I was being guided by God. I did not have the answers to what I would find in Scotland, but I had a feeling that this path was part of a mission that God had laid out for me. That gave me comfort as I readied for the journey of a lifetime.

It was in early September 1997 when, having made all my enquiries and got my mind focused on the journey into this unknown land, I made the ten-mile trip from San Juan to Piarco International Airport in a state of nervous anticipation. I had set aside my reservations by the time I said farewell to my family and friends with the plane ticket in my hand. It had been purchased for me by Mr Nafziger at a cost of £700, which was a month's wages for me. The prospect of playing in Scotland had been unimaginable, but I was excited as I boarded the plane with my ultimate destination being Glasgow. Things seemed to have happened so quickly. Just a few weeks earlier, I was content and anticipating a long career at Carib. Now, as I sat on the plane heading for new horizons, I wondered what lay ahead for me. It was an adventure and perhaps more than that. I was opening up a whole new chapter in my life. I looked out of the window as the plane took to the air, watching Trinidad disappear behind me. Scotland awaited.

In many ways, I regretted leaving the Carib Brewery but, as it turned out, things were about to change there. Mr Nafziger fell out with the bosses and left the company after I had gone. The new management was not as supportive of the team as he had been and I am sure that life would have been different afterwards had I stayed. I never knew about the prospective change when I left, but it seems that I had seen the best of times at Carib.

I often reflect on the vital role Mr Nafziger played in my career. Indeed, he had been an important character in the evolution of my life. Recently, I discovered that Jack Warner also had an involvement in my move. I had turned down his offer to join Joe Public, but he had not disappeared. I do not know exactly how he got involved, but it did not surprise me, knowing something about how football administration worked in Trinidad at that time. As the plane touched down under the grey skies at Glasgow Airport, I was ready for the adventure. I knew that I was to be collected by a former footballer, but I knew nothing of him. It was simply a case of getting through passport control, then collecting my luggage. My adventure would really start then. The first stop on my footballing journey in Scotland would be a town called Motherwell.

Chapter Four

A New Life, a New Land

IN THE Glasgow Airport arrivals hall, I was met by Stevie Archibald, the famous Scottish international player. He had played most notably with Tottenham Hotspur and Barcelona, having started his career in rather modest circumstances with Clyde. After hanging up his boots, he had become player-manager at East Fife and led them to promotion to the First Division. Early in the following season, he had a row with his board over funding and was sacked. He claimed the board at Methil did not match his ambition. In his time with them, he had acquired a couple of international players from Trinidad and Tobago – Arnold Dwarika and Craig Demmin – so he knew the scene on the islands and must have had good contacts. Dwarika had come from Joe Public, so perhaps the influence of Jack Warner was not so far away.

After he left management, Archibald acted as a consultant to agents in the transfer of players, presumably using his network of contacts. In my case, he was apparently acting as a front man on behalf of my appointed agent – a man named Majid Mohammad. I had never met Mohammad and I had never had or needed an agent before. This was all part of a new experience. Archibald was courteous with me and he probably had a greater sense of how I was feeling than most. He had once left the UK to play in Spain, so I imagined he might have had some sense of the change in culture I was facing. However, I imagined that travelling to Spain from Scotland was not the same culture change as coming from the Caribbean to Glasgow!

I knew that it had been arranged for me to go to Fir Park, the home of Scottish Premier Division club Motherwell. I did not know much about the club, but I trusted that they were a good team who could provide me with the chance I needed. They would have a look at me in training and matches to decide if my future lay with them. After Archibald had picked me up, he drove me straight to the bed and breakfast accommodation that would be my home for the duration of my time in the town. It was a decent place to stay and was run by a nice family. I would spend the night there before going into the ground next morning.

My first impressions having arrived in this new land were good. Everyone I had met so far was friendly but, after I laid my things down, my mind was racing as I tried to come to terms with what might lie ahead. That evening, I reflected on where the journey had taken me and all that had happened after I stepped on to the plane in Trinidad. Now I was sitting in a strange house, in a strange town, in a strange land and I wondered what I was letting myself in for.

The next morning, I was nervously excited when I was taken to Fir Park. Although it was not the most glamorous of stadia at that time and was far from being the biggest and best in Scotland, it was a revelation to me. I had only played in grounds like that in representative matches, so this had a sense of being in the 'big time'. In Trinidad, our club matches were played at small grounds which really did not compare. They might have one stand, but that was it. This was completely enclosed with stands.

I was introduced to the Motherwell manager, Alex McLeish, and he said that I was invited to stay for two weeks to give them a chance to assess me. I was shown into the dressing room and was handed some kit to get changed and ready to join the other players, who had started to arrive. I settled in and took part in training and, over the next few days, I played some trial matches. It was all pretty routine, but instead of heading back to my accommodation to be locked up until the next day, I found the Motherwell lads were friendly and keen to show me a bit of the local culture. They took me out on the town and my first visit to sample the night life was an evening at the Hamilton Palace nightclub. I had to adjust to the lingo, especially when they kept taking about 'birds', which I learned were young ladies and not the feathered variety!

One of the problems I faced in these early days was in simple communication. We all spoke English, but our accents were completely different. Coming from Trinidad, I spoke quickly and so did they, but with a Scottish twang. The first few conversations were punctuated with a few 'Eh?' 'What?' and puzzled expressions before we all got on the same wavelength.

At the end of the trial period, McLeish called me into his office to say that he had been impressed but that they would not be signing me. His comments to the press were complimentary and outlined Motherwell's position. He said: 'Marvin has marvellous assets in his game and I would have enjoyed working with him longer. However, he is not the finished article. He has tremendous potential, but we cannot afford and do not have the time to nurture him through. It's a shame, but there is nothing I can do about it and I wish him all the best.'

I knew he was right, because I did not know the Scottish game and I needed the time to mature, learn my profession and familiarise myself with this different style of playing. I was a little downcast, but I was not quite ready to head back to Trinidad. I knew that there were other opportunities. My agent spoke with the Raith Rovers manager, Jimmy Nicholl, and his assistant, Alex Smith. I was not completely unknown to that club, because they had signed a fellow Trinidad and Tobago international, Anthony Rougier, and he had done well for them. Indeed, he had moved to Hibs a couple of months earlier for a transfer fee of £250,000. I knew that if I could follow his example, I would do all right.

Alex McLeish (Former Manager at Motherwell FC and Rangers FC) – *Although he was young and very raw, Marvin had a presence and I thought tremendous potential. I could see he was not a 'Franz Beckenbauer' type and I am sure he would not disagree, but what a wonderful stopper he was. He was the archetypal centre-backs – the 'none shall pass' type who was very rugged and athletic, but I had to compare him with the centre-back that we had at the time in Chris McCart and Miodrag Krivokapić, who both provided more experience. However, I knew that Marvin would do a job for someone and could use his next move as a stepping stone for greater things.*

I knew that Raith Rovers had been relegated the previous season. It was a contrast in fortunes to what they had experienced just three years earlier. While still in the Scottish First Division, they had beaten Celtic in a penalty shoot-out to win the Coca-Cola Scottish League Cup at Ibrox Stadium in November 1994. That victory had given them a place in the UEFA Cup. They reached the second round of the competition and narrowly lost out to Bayern Munich. They also went on to win promotion to the Scottish Premier Division that season. It was a remarkable period for the club, but it had also come at a cost. They had lost a few of their key players and, after finishing mid-table in their first season in the Premier Division, they had slipped to the bottom in 1996/97 and were relegated.

That was not the only problem they faced that season. Lord Justice Taylor had been appointed to undertake an inquiry following the 1989 disaster at Hillsborough, Sheffield. One of his recommendations was that football clubs in the top tiers in both Scotland and England should have all-seater stadia. The deadline for compliance was August 1997 and Raith Rovers had embarked on a substantial redevelopment of Stark's Park, with new stands and seating at a cost of £2.3m. The work had been completed but it placed a significant financial burden on the club.

I travelled up to Kirkcaldy after Nicholl and Smith offered me a two-week trial. Nicholl was in his second spell at the club as manager, having rejoined a few months earlier. The club had been in some turmoil on and off the field. They had gone through four managers in 14 months, but there had then been a change in ownership at the club. That smoothed the way for Nicholl to return after turning down an earlier opportunity from the previous owner. Raith Rovers were essentially trying to rebuild after their halcyon days had ended and needed to be in the top flight to help haul themselves out of their financial mess.

I did not have international clearance to play in any organised fixtures, but I could play games behind closed doors. The club arranged a match against Dundee United at Tannadice and this would be my first chance. I remember it was very, very cold. It was frosty and the kind of cold I had never experienced before in my life. I had never seen a white pitch before and I could not understand how people would be expected to run around on such a surface. However, the United strikers managed it okay and kept running past me. By the end of the match, we had lost four goals without reply. I think one of the United players scored at least a hat-trick that day and I could not lay a glove on him. It was not my best game and I doubt if I impressed, but Nicholl said he would give me one last chance to prove myself in a match against Livingston at Almondvale.

By then, I was determined that this was the life I wanted to follow and I was desperate to impress. There was some added pressure, however. I was conscious that if the trials did not work out, I would be back in Trinidad with my tail firmly between my legs. Perhaps the chance of a move to professional football would never materialise again. The pressure was on, but I was up for it. As it turned out, I had a fantastic game that night in Almondvale, despite the weather being even colder than it had been in Dundee.

We won 2-0 and, immediately after the match, Jimmy came into the dressing room and said that the club were offering me a two-year contract. I would receive £500 per week. The decision was announced to the press and Alex Smith commented that I looked a player. He said: 'He is like a rock and we will have time to develop him here.' It was October 1997 and, at 21, I would sign my first professional contract. Raith Rovers of Scotland were my new team and I was delighted. I had reached a milestone in my career where I could properly call myself a professional footballer.

Jimmy Nicholl – (Former Manager of Raith Rovers) *– I received a call from a chap called Majid, who was a football agent based in Bradford. He told me that Alex McLeish had a player at Motherwell that would be available to me. I have no idea why he would select Raith Rovers unless we were just one of a number of clubs he called, but I invited him to ask Marvin to come up to Stark's Park so we could have a look at him. He played a couple of trial matches for us, but I recall him in training most of all.*

Even our own players hated playing against him, because he went through them all with solid robust challenges. He was a formidable big chap, who was frightened of nothing in a game. He was strong in the air and in the tackle, although his distribution wasn't the best. What I considered was whether his strengths would outweigh his weaknesses and on that basis we went ahead with the idea of him joining us. However, it was not a straightforward deal. By then I was speaking with a man called Jack Warner. I understood he was the owner of the club Marvin played with back in Trinidad – Joe Public. As it turns out, Marvin was not with Joe Public, but that is what I was led to believe. I told Walker that we wanted Marvin, but we had no money at Raith, so it was suggested that the deal be done based on any sell-on value, with the proceeds being split 50/50 between Raith Rovers and Jack Warner. The deal was concluded on that basis.

It was all subject to me getting international clearance, of course, and that would take a nervy three months. I would have to return to Trinidad before I could truly get into life at Stark's Park. All the time, I was hoping and praying that things would go smoothly in getting all the paperwork cleared to allow me to return to Kirkcaldy. The consequences of me not getting clearance were almost unthinkable. There was so much riding on it all that I could not bear to imagine any barrier to me becoming a professional footballer at Raith Rovers. The move would not only give me a chance to make something of a career in football, but it would generate money that would allow me to provide some support to my family back home. Only when the clearances were completed could I finally say farewell to my life on the island and look forward to the beginning of a new chapter.

I returned to Carib Brewery and remained with them until, thankfully, everything went through without a hitch. While I was back in Trinidad awaiting confirmation of my move, I continued to play with Carib FC. They were continuing to do well and, in the short spell I played with them when I returned, we won a cup. It was wonderful seeing all my friends from the brewery once again. When I received the necessary clearances to play in Scotland, my team-mates and friends in the company gave me a great send-off. I was really buzzing at the prospect of completing my signing for Raith Rovers.

So, it was back on a flight to Scotland, this time knowing a lot more about the country. I arrived in February 1998 and my contract with Raith Rovers was confirmed. Looking back at the situation now in the light of conversations with Jimmy Nicholl, it seems that the move was not particularly orchestrated by Carib, but by Jack Warner, who was using his network within the game. If I had known at the time, it would not have made any difference to me, but it did not surprise me. He had his fingers in many pies. It was an opportunity I could not turn down and concluding the deal was a dream.

Due to international commitments and a leg injury, it was a few weeks before I made my debut for Raith Rovers. I had been called up by Trinidad and Tobago to play in the Gold Cup tournament in California. However, after I flew back, I got a nasty infection in my leg. I had an abscess on my thigh that caused a massive swelling, necessitating an operation to cut it open, then clean out the infection. That left a hole in my leg which had to be protected by strapping to allow me to make my debut for Raith Rovers on 13 March 1998.

We ended up drawing the match 1-1 with Airdrie, but I felt I had done well. Certainly, Nicholl was happy with how I had performed and said: 'He has the attitude and determination to win the ball that we need.' It had gone well for me, but I found it so cold. I had never experienced this kind of weather in my life before, although I was told it was not the worst that could be thrown at us.

The following week, I helped the club get a great win against Falkirk at Brockville Park and a few nights later I played in my third match for the club, winning 4-1 against Hamilton Academicals. We were ten points behind the leaders Dundee, with just one promotion place up for grabs. It was disappointing that I could not have come into the team earlier and perhaps help close that gap.

For all the joy I experienced when I signed, I began to feel homesick. Until then, it had all been a fantasy, a dream to play at that level. However, when reality kicked in and I realised that I was thousands of miles from family and friends, it was tough. Although I got on well with the Raith players and had some good pals, it was a lonely time for me in the first few months, especially living and playing in what was a cold climate. I was used to the sun.

People who are accustomed to Scottish winters do not realise what it is like for those who are not. Playing in matches in these wintry conditions, when my hands were cold as ice, started to get to me. With a five-hour time difference between Scotland and Trinidad, I had a real sense of remoteness.

Scott Thomson (Former Team-mate at Raith Rovers) – *I remember when Marvin came in he was a rough diamond of a player, but you could see that he was going to be a great defender. We hated playing against him in training because he would go through you, especially if he was going for a header. He would stand on your toes, or even split your head in two, but always follow it up with – 'Sorry.' However, he was a brilliant character to have as a team-mate on and off the field, except when I was sharing a room with him at Linda and Harry's guesthouse. I would waken about 6.30am hearing Marvin mumbling his prayers. I said to him that we were not due to get up for another two hours so could he not wait until then? He said that 'God wakened him up' and I told him to ask God to waken me up at 9.00am!*

But he was good fun and even when we took him out at night on the town. One night Rossco (Ross Venables) and I decided we would try to get him drunk. He must have had about ten pints of Guinness and Rossco and I were both legless, but Marvin was half sober! There was no end to it, so we never did that again.

Similarly, he was insatiable when it came to food. We had a three-course meal every night at

On the beach at home in Trinidad

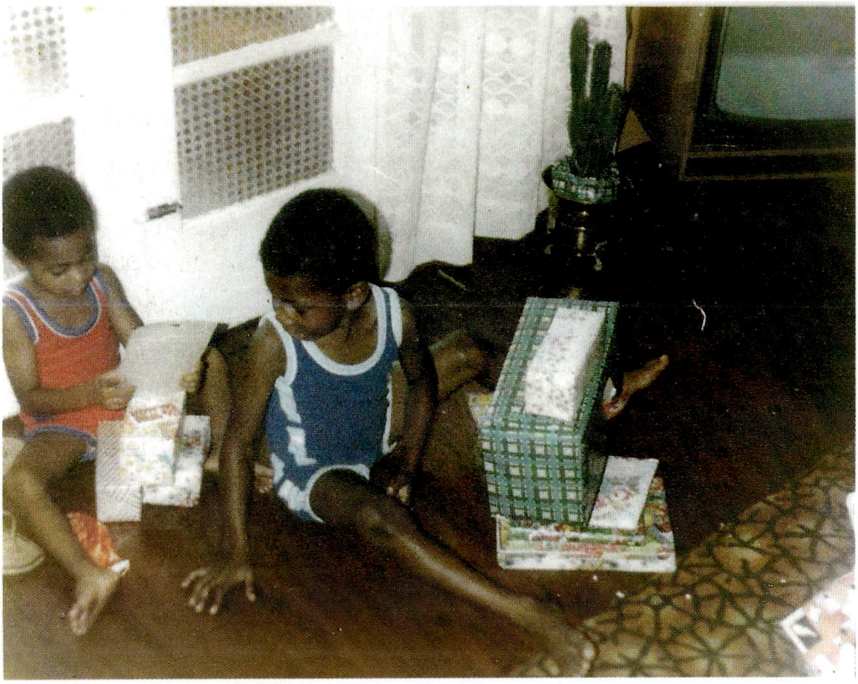

Micah and me at Christmas

My mother Cynthia with her grandchildren

Micah and me with our father Anthony

Me and Micah at the table

My grandmother Isidora

Me after making my first communion (centre) in church

My cousin (Stefan) and me

Anthony Rougier and me shortly after I arrived in Scotland

Me in my Trinidad and Tobago kit before the World Cup qualification CONCACAF game with the USA on 24 November 1996

Me preparing to officiate at a wedding ceremony

With Jason and Debbi Scotland after their wedding ceremony

'The Goalie' Andy Goram and me

Fernando Ricksen and me

Hibernian v Livingston. Hampden Park, Glasgow. Overjoyed Livingston players (from left): Roddy Mckenzie, Stuart Lovell, Derek Lilley, Oscar Rubio, Lee Makel and me celebrate winning the trophy

Bahrain midfielder Salman Isa, right, is chased by Trinidad and Tobago's Dennis Lawrence, left, Marvin Andrews, second left, and Silvio Spann during the first leg match of the qualifying play-off for the 2006 World Cup at the Hasely Crawford Stadium in Port-of-Spain, Trinidad, Saturday, 12 November 2005

Linda and Harry's', but even when we were finished he would still be hungry. Off we would then go to John Valente's fish and chip shop for a bag of chips. Despite it all, Marvin still had that chiselled physique. He was a great trainer and that seemed to deal with any food excess.

He was such an important player for us at Raith Rovers. Determined, but laid-back and that settled everyone. Everyone loved him and he was a great character to have around Stark's Park.

I was his personal chauffeur, or it seemed that way for most of the time I was in Kirkcaldy, but we built up a great friendship. In fact, although I only spent a year or so at Raith Rovers, that friendship has endured and we still keep in contact. He is a great guy and one that I am delighted to call a friend.

I could not drive at that time, so in the afternoons after training, I would go for a walk along the High Street, just to get me out. I was always conscious of people looking at me, because I was different to them. I never knew what they were saying or had any sense that they were making any negative comments, but it was a strange feeling. Eventually, I reached a stage where I thought that I would give it all up and return home. I even phoned my coach at Carib FC, Colin Murray, and told him I was thinking about coming back to Trinidad, but he talked me out of it, telling me to 'stick it out'. Deep down, I knew I would have to, but it was good to get that confirmation that this was for the best and I had to just live with it, at least until the weather turned. It would have meant giving up a great football opportunity that may not have arisen again. There really was no option, so I settled into this new life.

What helped me enormously in these first few difficult months was being accommodated in Linda and Harry Duffy's bed and breakfast. It was located right on Pratt Street, Kirkcaldy, directly opposite Rovers' Stark's Park ground. I would eventually live with them for four years and they virtually adopted me. Apart from being perfect hosts, they taught me all about the customs and traditions of the country and its history. In that first year, I enjoyed finding out about the culture. They even helped me adjust my diet to the typical Scots one. Besides haggis, which I tasted for the first time, they introduced me to fish and chips, which might be considered another new delicacy. Then there was Scotch broth. In Trinidad, we consider soup to be a meal in itself, with all sorts of things added, so Scottish soup took some time to get used to.

Linda and Harry provided me with a home and the family support that was so important to me at that stage in life in Scotland. I even used to call them 'mum' and 'dad', which is a measure of my relationship with them. The friendship they showed me was so touching, especially as a black person having his first personal contact with two white people. They highlighted how friendly and lovely Scottish people can be and they never once paid any attention to my colour or judged me because of my race. They saw me just as a human being and that helped me adjust and settle down in Kirkcaldy. It was the perfect introduction to Scotland and since that introduction to the town all these years ago, I have chosen to make it my home.

Besides the friendship that Linda and Harry provided, I also became close to other players who came to stay at the accommodation. Raith Rovers used the bed and breakfast to lodge others who arrived at the club. Sometimes these new guys would be put in beside me, sharing a room. They included Ross Venables and Scott Thomson, who had come from Aberdeen and went on to become a legend with Dunfermline Athletic. They used to make fun of my early rising at 6am to pray. That apparently woke them far earlier than they intended. Scott eventually asked for another room. I would also often read the Bible when they were watching TV, but they accepted that my faith was a major part of my life and that I needed to do these things. Although I must have frustrated them at times, they were both great friends during my time there.

Bob Malcolm (Former Team-mate at Rangers FC) – *I used to room with Marvin on away trips and once I woke up to him talking in his sleep – at least that's what I thought. However, it was very early in the morning and* *he was awake and reading the Bible. Hearing the story of the players who shared a room with him at Linda and Harry's, I have every sympathy!*

Day-to-day life in Scotland was something I would have to adjust to, but one of the major differences I found when I came to the country was in the football itself. As I mentioned, it was much faster that I had experienced in Trinidad and Tobago, where the whole way of life was so laid-back and even on the playing field, we started at a slow pace, knocking the ball around. The game was so frantic in Scotland that after five minutes I would have to catch my breath. It was more organised, too, and the system we played in when I arrived was a flat back four in a 4-4-2 set-up. I had never known that before. I was first and foremost a marker and played in front of a three-man defence. I had to adjust to that new role.

I even had to adjust to the simple things of the game like pre-match preparation, which most people in Scotland would take for granted. Back home, it was almost unheard of to have any kind of pre-match schedule or ritual. In Trinidad, players would turn up for a game when they liked, sometimes just in time for the kick-off. Life in the Caribbean is not driven by the clock. In Scotland, we had to operate to a schedule and I had to work to get used to that. A few times I was late, even though I lived just across the road from the ground.

I have to thank both Jimmy Nicholl and Alex Smith for being so tolerant until I got up to speed with the way of life. Jimmy was a wonderful character at the club. He had obviously become a local hero when he took the club to the League Cup and earned promotion to the Scottish Premier League. Of course, he had a wonderful CV on the playing side, too. A Northern Ireland international with 73 caps to his name, he had played as a full-back, most notably with Manchester United in the 1970s and early 1980s before eventually finding his way to Rangers. He had virtually signed off his playing career at Raith Rovers, going on to become boss.

Jimmy worked hard at creating a good atmosphere in training. He would mix up the hard work with some fun. We would play games like 'crossbar challenge', where all the players would try to strike the woodwork from outside the penalty area. He worked with me to help improve my game. As a former defender himself, he would advise on the positions I should take up for set pieces.

He was superb tactically and was extremely popular. Alex Smith also had a great track record, having guided both St Mirren and Aberdeen to some real success. He was very technical and I also learned a lot from him. I certainly improved as a defender under their influence.

Terry Butcher (Former Coach at Raith Rovers) – *When I saw Marvin at Raith Rovers, I knew he was very raw but I had no doubts that he would go on to have a* *great career in the game. When you look at players, you assess their positives against their negatives. Marvin was not great on the ground, but he was a colossus in the air and very quick. He looked a great talent and it was a pleasure to help coach him at that stage in these early years of his career.*

I even had guest coaching sessions from former Rangers and England captain Terry Butcher, who was on the backroom team. Although he was mostly involved in coaching the youngsters, he often gave me a bit of one-to-one guidance. I hadn't realised what a big-name player he was until afterwards. It was invaluable to learn from such a major figure in the game. Although I had good coaches, I knew I would have to learn the game in this new country for myself and I actually found that my style was well suited to Scottish football. I liked the physicality of the game, but I needed to learn to stay on the right side of the officials. Like most Trinidadian defenders, I was very fit, enthusiastic and aggressive. However, I was also raw and perhaps clumsy at times, which led to some run-ins with the referees, especially in my first few games. I started my career at Raith Rovers with four straight yellow cards and followed these up with a red. They were not malicious challenges, but I realised that I would need to adapt to the officials in Scotland as well as the Scottish game.

I did settle well into Scottish football, although I suffered more than a few bangs in physical challenges, especially in the air. In one match against Hibs, I ended up with one eye completely closed and the other stitched up. That was all part of the game and I relished these types of challenges. It was what I was used to in Trinidad, where we are trained to be hard, fearless challengers for the ball.

I felt I was doing well with Raith Rovers, but players always need reassurance. I received that when Nicholl told me he had not expected me to be such a valuable player. It was a great lift at an important stage in my development. I had warmed to the club and the fans embraced me. I knew, though, that the club's financial worries were running deep. The need to provide an all-seater ground in order to operate in the newly established Scottish Premier League was crippling and achieving promotion was vital. The new league structure had embraced the findings of the Taylor Report. The inauguration of the new league would be the 1998/99 season, less than a year after I had arrived. The club had done all it could and the ground would satisfy the criteria for the new league. However, the club had to get there first.

Jimmy Nicholl (Former Manager at Raith Rovers) – *Even though Marvin lived just across the road he and Scott Thomson ('Nipper') were always late. He told me that Marvin's early-morning prayers and singing had caused him to sleep in! I suggested he set his alarm* *for 8.45am, but Nipper said it would be easier telling God to awaken him at that time, since he seemed to control the alarm in their room! Marvin was just Marvin and we had to put up with the timekeeping issue at the start, although it got better. He was an instant hit in the dressing room and became a huge player for us.*

He had a tremendous ability with his head and we even got wise to that, using it to counter-attack teams. He would head the ball a good 40 yards or so and that always put the opposition on the back foot.

We worked on him defensively, too. I had Terry Butcher doing a stint once a week with the younger boys and he would occasionally take Marvin aside. I was not sure how far he would go in the game unless his distribution improved, but I thought he had everything else to make it as a top player.

He was a really engaging guy and even when things got tough financially for Raith and we asked the players to take a cut, Marvin pleaded that it would make things difficult for him, because he sent his money home for his family. That is the kind of man he is.

Sadly, despite completing the major stadium revamp in good time to allow them to play in the elite league, Raith Rovers had been relegated the year before I joined. That was a hammer blow to them when they really needed the money to pay back the loan. They would have to play in the Scottish First Division, but they retained their ambitions to get promoted right away into the new Scottish Premier League. They remained full-time and, with a squad of around 30, the annual wage bill, combined with the stadium debt, was constricting. As a consequence, they never made any real inroads to the debt level.

Raith Rovers needed to be in the Premier League to benefit from the big gates that visits from the likes of the Old Firm would generate at Stark's Park. Our failure to take that step up had a critical impact upon the club's financial position. Memories of that famous League Cup win in 1994 – and the taste of Europe that followed – remained fresh. However, for all that the club were keen to maintain that kind of success, they had to sell their players to remain afloat. They could only survive by selling their most valuable assets.

Most of the heroes from that cup campaign had been moved on and the club had to rebuild while still pursuing promotion. It was a catch-22 situation. They had to keep recruiting well so they could continue to generate funds by selling on their discoveries. That was why their model of recruiting players like me, who were seasoned internationals but relatively unknown, worked well for them. We cost next to nothing but could spin the club a decent transfer fee.

I understood the situation and if it helped Raith Rovers to maintain their ambitions by selling me on, then it was also good for me. The club had given me a platform to show what I could do in the Scottish game and I would help in any way I could.

We just missed out on promotion in my first season in Scotland. Our away record was poor and that killed our hopes, but we were up against it in any case. Dundee had new owners who poured money into the club and they won promotion with a squad that was completely revamped with some great signings. There were just 11 games left in the title race when I made my debut. I felt I played well in the run-in and I even scored four goals, but we missed out on promotion, finishing third behind champions Dundee and second-placed Falkirk. The team had been inconsistent but we discovered some form over the last few games and there was a lot of hope that the next season would bring better fortune.

The optimism that followed after our tilt at promotion in 1997/98 quickly dissipated, however. Our hopes were left in tatters after only a few games and, rather than fighting for promotion, we ended up battling relegation from the First Division. At the end of January 1999, the team were third bottom and we heard the club faced possible bankruptcy. It was hard to concentrate in games knowing that the club could close at any time. The directors were looking to move players on and recoup money where possible. I was sent down to Doncaster Rovers for a trial, with a £75,000 price tag on my head. The prospective move did not materialise but, with the club in deep financial trouble, I knew I would have to go eventually. I was happy to remain with Raith Rovers for as long as they needed me but I would leave if the right deal for them came along.

The fans were not happy with the situation or the performances that followed and attendances began to dwindle. We had given them little to shout about. It reached an all-time low when we lost 6-0 at home to St Mirren, but there were further worries ahead for me. Aside from the concern over the club's financial woes, I was still enjoying life at Raith Rovers and in Kirkcaldy, but then I suffered an injury. I pulled a groin and it developed into an inflammation of my pelvis bone. This was a complication which I put down to training on heavier grounds than I had been used to. It was an injury that never went away. I would play without pain one week, then break down the next. I was worried that if I constantly broke down in matches, my future in Scotland would be bleak. If I could not play regularly, I might find myself out of football altogether. I did not want to end up being cast on the scrap heap and on a flight home to Trinidad.

I was advised by the medical practitioners who examined me at the hospital that they could give me tablets for the inflammation, but that I would likely need an operation, with a metal plate being installed in my abdomen. That was what led me to the door of Pastor Joe Nwokoye, as I explained earlier. Prior to that, I had never been to a church in Scotland before, but the recommendation from Anthony Rougier opened the door to the Zion Praise Centre in the town.

Back at the club, the physiotherapists had me on the treatment table and said they wanted me to go under the knife. I told them this would not be necessary as I would rely on God to help me through my injury. They were surprised and probably a bit concerned, but that was the course I followed. Then, one morning, I awoke and the pain was gone. I suffered no further setbacks with the injury and I continued playing through to the end of the season. Not only that, but I won the supporters' Player of the Year award next season.

The doctors were astounded and, although some have claimed that it was mind over matter, there is little doubt in my mind that it was my faith and God which healed me. It was my first step in realising that prayer could heal a physical problem. At the time, there was not a lot made of it in the press because I was not a well-known player.

Later, of course, my experiences with my knee leading up to Helicopter Sunday gained widespread coverage, but this first experience was not known to them. I was still relatively unknown and it was probably of little interest to the press. It was a matter solely between me and the club, but for me it was a huge turning point in my life. Although I had a Christian upbringing and prayed a lot for protection of my family, the experience of God's role in my healing left a huge impression on me. I resolved that I would become more active in the church and it would be a central part of my life.

The club survived in the First Division in 1998/99, finishing third bottom, but the disappointment over the team's performances saw Jimmy Nicholl and Alex Smith dismissed, as their contracts expired in June 1999. Their departure was a bit untidy, as Raith unveiled a new management team of John McVeigh and Peter Hetherston before things had been settled with Jimmy and Alex.

Our away record had been the real killer – we won just three games on the road. Decent players left the club as another rebuild began for a renewed shot at promotion. As far as Nicholl and Smith were concerned, I had to thank them for giving me that first opportunity and opening the door to a new life. Had they not given me another chance after that first poor trial at Dundee United, then I might well have had to return home. They did all they could to manage the club out of its financial woes. They had even taken a significant wage cut at the end of January 1999 and the players also decided to waive their win bonuses for the season. As Jimmy highlighted, the fans had done their bit in trying to help the club, digging deep for all sorts of fundraising schemes. He felt that it was only right that the players and management team do so, too. Ultimately, the pressures weighed heavily on us and although we survived in the division, the club needed more than that.

As far as the upcoming season was concerned, I waited to see how the new management team would be and what lay ahead of me. It was obvious to everyone that we needed a new approach. Almost as soon as McVeigh and Hetherston took over, we were defending better and looked more likely to score. There was a lot of talent in the squad and some of the players went on to better things, but the underlying financial problems remained.

In December 1999, McVeigh was on his way after just five months in the hot seat. We were fourth in the table at the time and had already gathered the same number of points the club had achieved in the whole of the previous season. The chairman commented that the board had taken the decision to sack McVeigh for reasons not related to the team's performances. No formal reason was given for his departure, and we were left largely in the dark. At least there was some continuity when his assistant, Peter Hetherston, reluctantly agreed to take over as caretaker boss. Kenny Black, who had coached the youths, was given the opportunity to work alongside him.

All we could do in the dressing room was to continue to show the spirit that McVeigh had instilled in us. It was the least we could do to support Peter and we got him off to a good start with a 4-2 win against Inverness Caledonian Thistle. That win probably secured the job for Peter and we did well for the remainder of the season, but still only finished in mid-table.

In the spring, with Raith pursuing promotion, I had to turn my attention away from the domestic scene as Trinidad and Tobago embarked on their quest for qualification for the 2002 World Cup. Since 1998, the team had been known as the 'Soca Warriors'. The term Soca came from 'Soul-Calypso', which was a popular musical genre. It was a nickname we were proud to be given, just as the 'Strike Squad' had been proud of their nickname a decade earlier.

I was called up for every match, six qualifiers over a ten-week period from March to May 2000. I had made no secret of how important it was for me and my country to make the finals, but it did not help Raith Rovers' cause. They were desperate for points and it seemed that when they really needed me for vital matches, I was called away on international duty. We had opened our World Cup qualification campaign well, comfortably progressing to through to the crucial final group stage. Indeed, I had scored the first goal of the campaign when we defeated Dutch Antilles, playing under our new manager, Ian Porterfield. He had bossed both Aberdeen and Chelsea in his career before going on to manage in some more far-reaching football outposts. Hetherston's aggravation with my international commitments was exacerbated when I was also called up for friendly matches.

He was very frustrated, especially as Raith's quest for promotion faltered. He said: 'Marvin is a key player for us and it is my opinion that had we had him for the whole season, we would have been set for promotion.' It was a problem that would continue into the next season as we continued to progress in the World Cup qualification process.

The club had no alternative but to let me go whenever I was called up, as they could have been hit with a fine, which was the last thing they needed. It all put me in a difficult club versus country dilemma that I had no control over. Issues of trust began to arise when I missed a connecting flight back home and was delayed in Miami. The carnival was on in Trinidad at the time and I was accused of deliberately missing the plane so I could hop over to enjoy the celebrations. It was nonsense. I did not leave Miami. I had told the club the truth, as I always would, that I simply missed the flight. They should have realised that I do not tell lies. On another occasion, Raith had a crucial match against rivals Dunfermline coming up and Hetherston called Porterfield to ask if I could be withdrawn from the national squad. He declined, which seemed double standards given that Russell Latapy, Tony Rougier and Dwight Yorke had all been allowed to miss the international. Trinidad and Tobago's reasoning was that they did not have cover for me, but I know that Raith were frustrated and I felt helpless. They believed the system favoured the bigger clubs, who had greater sway over the national associations than lowly Raith Rovers.

The club versus country problem had festered with Raith Rovers for some time and even a couple of years earlier it prompted the club to announce they would no longer sign foreign players who might be required for international duty. They thought it was unfair to be paying the wages of a player who was away a lot on international duty, which was understandable.

At the end of the season, I had much to consider. The situation at Raith Rovers was unsettling, with the debt level suggested to be around £1m. I had to maintain a focus on my ambitions at this time. I was about to go out of contract and, still aged just 24, it was a critical stage in my career, as well as my life. From what had been going on at Stark's Park, it seemed that my future could lie elsewhere and I knew I had to look at every option. I was aware that there had been interest from other clubs. Dwight Yorke was extremely helpful at that time, giving me good advice on selecting the right club and what terms to expect, as well as recognising how my own spirituality fitted around all of that. Dwight had played at the top in England and, like him, I also wanted to play against the best players. I was intrigued and naturally attracted by the possibility of a move to the FA Carling Premiership in England. That would have been perfect, but it seemed more likely that I would remain in Scotland.

Potential moves within Scotland were beginning to materialise and there was speculation that I might be off to Aberdeen, with a transfer fee of £100,000 suggested. The prospect of me joining the Dons caused a bit of amusement in our dressing room. The players started talking in the Doric, which was even harder to understand than the Fife dialect! They also spoke about sheep, but I was completely unaware of what they were on about!

I had a natural desire to play against better players and further my career, but I was entirely happy at Raith Rovers. For all the financial worries surrounding the club, I had no reason to move on a personal level. The fans had been great with me and I had made many friends in Kirkcaldy. I kept my head down and continued to perform as well as I could for the team. I was even getting among the goals and scored two in a great 4-0 win at Almondvale against Livingston in September 2000. The first was a header but, uncharacteristically, the second came with my foot, as I slid the ball into the net. It was only the second goal I had scored with my foot and the victory it helped secure was huge for us. Livingston were hot favourites to take the championship and we had destroyed them that day. I did not realise, but it had also made an impact on the Livingston management.

Life was good, but the seriousness of the club's position was never far away from our minds. It all reached a critical stage for me in September 2000. The chairman took me aside one day after training and said that, although he wanted me to stay, if I remained with the club they did not know if they would be able to pay my wages the next month. That really brought it home that my future probably would not be at Stark's Park.

I did not know that one of the clubs that had been monitoring my situation were Livingston. I imagine that there were a lot of conversations going on behind the scenes with different clubs, although no one mentioned to me what interest there had been. A couple of weeks or so later, after the chairman had made clear the harsh realities of the club's financial position, the situation took another turn. I came in for training and, along with Steven Tosh and Alex Burns, was called into the chairman's office. He told us not to train but to get ourselves over to Livingston because they wanted to sign us. It was all very sudden but, having endured the uncertainty of the situation at Raith Rovers for some time, we welcomed the news. In fact, on hearing it was Livingston who were in for us, we were excited. The move was a bit of a dream for me because there was a lot of interest in what was happening at Livingston at the time. They were clearly an ambitious club and were seemingly cash-rich, with money being poured in by directors Dominic Keane and John McGuinness, a superfan who had won the lottery. McGuinness had apparently injected £4m into the club. They were committed to winning the league and gaining promotion to the Scottish Premier League.

So, the three of us made the 40-mile journey down to Livingston to meet our prospective new employers. There had been no negotiations that involved any of us. It seemed that it had all been decided between the clubs and we were on our way.

The club had been formed from the original Meadowbank Thistle and the owners had seen the potential of relocating them to the 'new town' of Livingston. It seemed a fertile base for gathering a new band of supporters. It was an exciting time to be at the club, with their new stadium and high ambitions. They had marched up through the lower leagues and needed to make the final step up to the Scottish Premier League to complete an amazing journey. This was the thrust of what both Keane and manager Jim Leishman said when I met them. They were both impressive individuals with a clear vision of what they wanted for the club and from me. New players were being added and there was certainly a buzz around the club and the town.

When we looked around the set-up at Livingston's Almondvale ground, we were impressed. I wanted to be part of it and it was clear they were keen for me to be part of the team. Leishman said he had been watching me for some time and that he had a vision for how he wanted to use me in his team. He was extremely persuasive and even came along to one of my prayer meetings and heard an American gospel choir. He said the experience was humbling and that he admired my faith and belief. It was good that he showed so much interest in me and my life that he took the trouble to seek out my church.

Jim Leishman (Former Livingston Manager)– *The first time I saw Marvin at Raith Rovers my first* *impressions were that he was okay – a good defender and not a bad centre-half. I never saw him again for some time, until Livingston met them again in the First Division on 16 September 2000. Marvin scored the first goal with a header and Raith won 4-0. I realised then that he had definite potential!*

The final negotiations on the transfer of the three of us were conducted quickly and professionally. We moved in a deal that the newspapers said was worth £100,000 to Raith Rovers. My wages were raised to £1,500 a week and I imagine the others got an increase too, so everyone was happy – except Peter Hetherston and the fans back in Kirkcaldy. The Raith directors met them at Stark's Park and explained that if we had not been sold, the club would have faced liquidation. The fans threatened to boycott every home game, but it was extremely difficult for the club, who I gathered needed £100,000 every month until the end of the season to survive. With gates falling, they were only taking in around £15,000 per week, so drastic action was needed. The club considered they would need another £400,000 by June, so the outlook was bleak.

I felt sorry for Hetherston, who was depressed over the situation, but we had at least given the club a lifeline. For me, it would be a new turn in the journey of my life in Scotland and I looked forward optimistically. Livingston, under manager Leishman, had great plans and an ambition to make it to the top flight. The club had only been formed four years earlier, but everything was geared towards promotion to the Scottish Premier League and I wanted to be part of their story.

Chapter Five

The Soca Warrior Joins the Livi Lions

I SIGNED for Livingston on 28 September 2000 and made my debut alongside my former Raith team-mates a week later, celebrating with a 3-1 win over Ross County. I was delighted with my performance and the nice comments that Jim Leishman made after the game. He said: 'He's a smashing footballer and a smashing person.' I was very happy and had a good feel about the club in its nice new stadium at Almondvale.

The team were nicknamed the 'Livi Lions', which was apt because we feared no one and would fight to beat the best. They would have no worries in that regard from me. It typified the spirit that had been embodied in me and I would battle for them as I did for every team I played for. The season had started well, although we were contesting the top spot with Falkirk, who had beaten Livingston a couple of days after I joined. However, from that first victory over Ross County, the team went on an unbeaten run right up to mid-January. We overcame a setback, a defeat against Falkirk, and by March we had virtually sealed promotion. The challenge from 'The Bairns' was short-lived and had faded.

Ultimately, we won the title in convincing fashion, finishing seven points clear of our nearest rivals, Ayr United. The title was sealed with a hard-fought 3-2 win at Inverness and our delighted fans celebrated on the pitch as we were presented with the trophy. Now, everything was geared towards the Scottish Premier League.

It was a huge achievement for the club and a great reward for all the hard work and investment that had gone into reaching this stage in the club's short history. We had been the club everyone was talking about in the First Division but the following season, 2001/02, we would be the underdogs. We would be playing against the big Scottish sides including Rangers and Celtic, but I relished the opportunity to play at that level. I was sure that the top teams would not underestimate us. They knew that we would be no pushovers, because we had gained some big Premier League scalps in cup ties while we were still in the First Division. We had knocked Aberdeen out of the Scottish Cup in a replay at Pittodrie to book a place in the quarter-finals. We could only manage a draw with 'The Dons' in the first match at Almondvale and they were expected to make no mistake at Pittodrie. However, that night we defended well and frustrated them. Then, with just eight minutes to go, we took our chance when Scott Crabbe headed what would turn out to be the winner.

The win gave us some respectability among the big sides because Aberdeen were a club with a great tradition, but we had taken the game to them and won. Aberdeen frequently challenged for the big prizes and had reached the finals of the Scottish Cup and League Cup a season earlier, so it was undoubtedly a big result for us.

We went on to comfortably eliminate Peterhead but sadly lost out 3-0 to Hibernian in the semi-finals. The margin of the scoreline was not a fair reflection of that game, but we had already shown we could compete with the top teams in Scotland.

After gaining promotion, the team was boosted with the arrival of four new Spanish players, including David Fernandez. He had once played for Deportivo La Coruña before Stevie Archibald used his Spanish contacts to lure him to Airdrie. Fernandez was to prove to be a great goalscorer and got us off to the perfect start in the Premier League, netting the winner against Hearts at Almondvale in our first match of the campaign. Another Spaniard who joined us through the same Archibald-inspired route was goalkeeper Francisco Javier Sánchez Broto. He came with great credentials too, having played with the likes of Zaragoza and Villarreal. Besides the Spaniards, we also had players from Italy, Togo, France, Argentina, Canada and Jamaica. It was truly multi-national but, since we had all arrived at this club with a sense of adventure, we were bonded by unity and positivity. In many ways, we all felt we had something to prove and that gave us an added edge in games.

That win against Hearts, who were a decent side, silenced some of the critics who had us marked down as also-rans in the title race. We quickly gained respect and we had that little extra bit of inspiration after hearing some condescending media coverage. One media hack called us a 'pub team' and another 'Johnny-come-latelys', but it did not take them long to realise we were a formidable outfit. The Old Firm would soon find that out, too.

After our win against Hearts, we travelled to Ibrox the next week to play against the famous Glasgow Rangers. It would be my first visit to the ground. As our team bus pulled up to the frontage on Edmiston Drive, I was amazed. At first, I didn't even think it was a stadium, as its red-brick façade looked very grand. As we got off the bus and walked in through the front doors, we were welcomed by a commissionaire. Inside, I was in awe as I looked at the two tall pillars in the entrance hall and the marble staircase. My reaction was Wow! Even going along to the dressing room, I was amazed, looking around at all the wood panelling. This was like nothing I had experienced anywhere else.

When we went out through the tunnel and on to the pitch, I was stunned when I looked around at the stands. I was taken aback by the sheer size of the stadium. Back in the Caribbean, the grounds were small and had, at most, just small stands on each of the four sides. This arena was something else. I was eager to get my kit on and get on with the game. Just before kick-off, we got the call to take to the field and when I ran out on to the pitch, I found the whole experience truly mind-blowing. There were almost 50,000 fans in the stands, almost all wearing blue and cheering on their club.

The Rangers team had the likes of Fernando Ricksen, Bert Konterman, Claudio Caniggia, Tore André Flo and Neil McCann in their line-up. Even on the bench they had great stars like Michael Mols and Andrei Kanchelskis. I had never played on a stage like that before and I was nervous as hell. However, I was determined to play well. It was always my philosophy that when you play these big matches, they provide a wonderful opportunity to show that you can play at that level. I saw it as a chance to make an impression on people. My prayer to God was a simple one – help me play well and perform well. After we were promoted, a lot of people had written us off. This was our chance to show that we deserved to be in the Scottish Premier League, playing against the top sides. Rangers certainly fell into that category.My nerves had disappeared quickly and I was enjoying playing in front of this crowd. I quickly settled into the game, making some hefty challenges on the home side's star attackers. I was determined to leave an impression on them, as a tough defender should. My immediate opponent was Flo and I handled him well before he was replaced by Mols. Again,

I held my own and we managed to hold Rangers to a 0-0 draw. The point we won was a huge one, even at that early stage of the season. Psychologically, I felt that if we could live with Rangers at Ibrox, then no one would take us for granted. I left the ground satisfied with my day's work, but I never imagined at that time that eventually I would play for the Light Blues at this wonderful stadium.

My Trinidad and Tobago team-mate Russell Latapy should have been in the Ibrox side that afternoon, but he claimed he had got caught up in traffic and missed the game, which angered Rangers manager Dick Advocaat. I have to say that of all the great footballers I have played with through my career, I would regard Latapy the best technically. He often had a problem over his commitment and I am sure that if he had always shown the desire and urgency that is needed, he would have been considered one of the game's great players.

Two weeks after drawing with Rangers, we held Celtic to a goalless draw at Almondvale. Jim Leishman said I had been 'outstanding' against John Hartson. Henrik Larsson had missed a penalty near the end as I turned away and prayed. I must give credit to our goalkeeper, Sánchez Broto, who saved brilliantly, but my comments afterwards caused some stir in the press room. One of the hacks asked me what would have happened if Larsson also prayed. I said that 'God would have answered the person who believes more!' That created some great headlines like 'Marvin's Prayers Answered', 'God Saved Us' and

'Livi's God Squad'. It all made me happy because having that profile after a big match had helped me project my testimony on the power of prayer to a wider audience. I was beginning to be known for more than football.

By the end of October, we had lost just once in the league and we were regularly playing in front of 10,000 fans at Almondvale. It was good to see that our solid start was fulfilling the club's ambitions and being rewarded with good local support. I was making big money now, but I did not forget my roots. I sent boots and strips to my old club back in Trinidad to help the youngsters show their talent and seize the opportunities I was now enjoying. I hoped it might inspire them so that they might follow in the footsteps of the likes of Latapy, Yorke and myself.

I had started the 2001/02 season well and I was voted SPL Player of the Month for August. However, just a few days before I received the award, I was caught up in the horrific events of the 9/11 terrorist atrocities. I was watching television when all the channels turned to the dreadful events as they unfolded in New York, when passenger planes were flown into the twin towers of the World Trade Center. My father worked in a hospital in Manhattan, just a short distance from the scene. I was immediately gripped with concern and I tried unsuccessfully to call him. I had to endure several anxious hours until I managed to get him on the phone. I discovered that he had been on his way out of Manhattan when the planes struck, so he was safe. My thoughts were with all those who could not get the reassurance I received that day. The following year, I made my own pilgrimage to 'ground zero'. It was a humbling moment.

After going eight games undefeated in the league, we welcomed Rangers to Almondvale in October 2001. This time, it was not a happy experience for me, as I conceded a penalty for a late challenge in the penalty box on Flo. For that, I also received a red card and, although Flo missed the penalty, it was not a good day all round. Rangers won comfortably 2-0, with Claudio Reyna scoring both goals.

Despite that setback, I felt I had performed well in my introduction to the Premier League and, by December, both Celtic and Rangers, along with some clubs in England, were apparently interested in signing me. My contract was due to expire in May 2002, which left Livingston trying to tie me to an extension. I was flattered by the interest from other clubs but Livingston had been good to me and I had no real inclination to move on. In the first week of December 2001, I had a chat with Jim Leishman and the club offered me a two-year contract with a one-year option that would take me up to 2005. Before I had committed to the deal, I had deliberated over the possibility of a move, but I prayed to God to guide me and I also spoke with Pastor Joe. I remained convinced that God had not finished with the things he would do with me at Livingston and the decision thereafter was an easy one. Perhaps the opportunities for a move to a big club would come in the future but, for now, my commitment would be to Almondvale.

I confirmed to Leishman that I would sign the contract extension and he was delighted. He told the assembled press: 'It is magnificent news for everyone involved at the club. The chairman, the fans and the players are delighted. It also demonstrates the faith he has in the club.' Livingston were clearly happy with the news and I was also delighted to remain with them. Another reason I was comfortable committing to the club was that they had managed my international commitments without any quibbles. They had released me without question to play for Trinidad and Tobago whenever I was called up. That was important to me as I continued my quest to reach the 2002 World Cup finals in Japan and South Korea.

The new deal I signed with Livingston pushed my wages up to £3,000 per week. I felt like a millionaire and I continued to send money back to my family in Trinidad, as I had done since I arrived in Scotland. I certainly felt like I was in the big time and the team continued to surpass expectations. We had more than held our own in the title race and good wins against the likes of Aberdeen, Hearts and even Rangers showed that we were a good side. The 2-1 win over the Ibrox side was particularly impressive as we had gone behind after just four minutes. But a good goal from Barry Wilson and then a fabulous bicycle kick from Stuart Lovell in the final minute sealed an important three points for us.

A fine victory at Tynecastle in the final game of the season clinched third place for us behind Rangers and Celtic, who won the title. The cup competitions did not offer the same joy, but our league position secured us a place in the qualifying rounds of the UEFA Cup. It was a remarkable journey for a club that was just seven years old. I had established myself in the team as one of the club's key players and life was good.

Our European adventure that next season began with a trip to Liechtenstein's FC Vaduz. We defeated them on the away goals rule to set up a tie against Austrian side Sturm Graz in the first round proper. We effectively lost the tie with a 5-2 defeat in the first leg in Austria before losing 8-6 on aggregate. I had been ruled out of the first leg with a knee injury but I returned for the second leg and managed to get a goal as we went on to win 4-3. It was a brave performance and underlined the progress the club had made in a short time.

After our spirited performance in the league in 2001/02, the lustre faded from our performances the following season. We lost both Javier Sánchez Broto and David Fernandez to Celtic, the latter moving in a transfer worth £1.5m. The fire had gone out of some of our performances. We slipped in the league and ended up battling relegation, finally managing to finish safely in ninth place. Had I not scored with two minutes to go to give us a 1-0 win against Dundee United at Tannadice on 15 May 2003, we would have been relegated. I saw the space opening up in front of me and, with time running out, I decided to push forward with the ball. My run took me all the way into the United penalty area and, when the keeper came out to close me down and direct me away from the goal, I stuck out my leg to knock the ball past him. It was the last of the four goals I scored for the club that season and none was more important.

If the league season had been troublesome, the cup competitions offered no respite. We exited the Scottish Cup in the third round at the hands of Dunfermline Athletic, while Dundee United terminated our progress in the League Cup at the quarter-final stage. The optimism and joy that surrounded the club in its first season in the SPL was replaced by concern and pessimism. If things were not going so well on the field for the team, the club had greater worries off it. It seemed that the spending that fuelled Livingston's ambitions had begun to catch up with it. The frustrations behind the scenes extended to the backroom, and manager Jim Leishman got involved in an altercation with a fourth official in a match against Dundee in March. He was fined by the SFA and banned from the touchline for 12 matches.

At the end of the season, Leishman moved upstairs, becoming director of football, allowing Márcio Máximo to come in as the new manager. He had been the Brazilian Under-17 coach and had introduced the Brazilian superstar Ronaldo to international football. Máximo would be the first Brazilian to manage a football team in the UK. Some of his methods were unconventional and he had to adapt to the Scottish style of play. I guess it all started to go wrong for him in his very first training session with us. He came out with this big bag of tennis balls and then proceeded to hand one to each of us. He then had us doing keepie uppies with tennis balls. A lot of the guys just looked at him. Some even began to wonder if he was actually qualified. It was then that some of the other coaches began to wonder what he was about. He also tried to get our fitness up a few notches and training became arduous, with three sessions a day.

The changes he instigated were quite radical and there is no doubt that he introduced many good ideas in his coaching. He tried to add more flair to the team, making the tactics more fluid and less rigid. However, although his communication with the players was good, some of them struggled to take his ideas on board. The other coaches were not on the same page either. In a sense, we understood the need to change, but it undoubtedly created some conflicts behind the scenes. We were aware of some arguments he had with the Scottish coaches, who also had their own conflicts. That did not create the harmony the team needed at that time. We tried to work through it and although there were problems, we were shocked when Máximo decided to leave after just four months. He cited personal reasons for his decision.

He had been in charge for just nine games. We had won only three of them. The chairman was disappointed with his departure and, although the results were disappointing, he was at great pains to point out that there had been no pressure from the board.

The club's financial woes continued and in August 2003, just before Máximo's departure, Livi looked to move me on when Dundee United showed interest. I was one of the highest earners at the club and it was speculated that I could command a big transfer fee. If I moved on, it would provide a valuable cash injection for the club and obviously remove me from the wage bill. The Tannadice side had offered Livingston a transfer fee of £250,000, which had been accepted, and my wages would rise to £3,500 a week. It seemed that everyone was happy, but before any move would take place, I had to satisfy myself that it would be a good one for me. A meeting was organised up at Dundee, but I did not attend. The players had arranged a day at Chester races and, even though I do not bet, I joined them for a fun day out. In a way, that decision indicated that I was not wholly committed to the idea of the move.

Another meeting was arranged and the night before I travelled up to meet them, I could not sleep as I deliberated over the move. As I had done before, I prayed for God's guidance in making the right decision for me. Having slept on it, I was consumed with the belief that this was not the move for me. It was my belief that God had used his guiding hand in my decision. I would not sign for Dundee United.

That day, I went up to Tannadice to meet United manager Ian McCall and chairman Eddie Thompson. They fully expected me to sign, but I sat down with them and gave them the news. I said that I had always told them that God would help me decide on the right path for my career and I had chosen to stay at Livingston. They were astonished and their chairman later said that he usually got what he wanted, but that in this case he could not compete with God. I simply did not feel this was the right move for me and I did not get a good feeling about the chairman either. On the face of it, the move might have seemed a good one for me, but I knew that, by turning down the opportunity, I was taking the right path. I was at peace with my decision.

I just wanted to be part of Livingston Football Club because of what they had been through and the great years that I had had with them. Jim Leishman, Davie Hay and Dominic Keane had all transformed the club and my heart was with them. I knew that, at some point, God would have a different plan for me but, for the moment, I knew I had made the right decision to remain with Livi.

There were headlines like 'God is not a Tangerine', reflecting the Tannadice side's shirt colour, but this was not about Dundee United. It was the path I had to take. McCall was disappointed, but he said that he respected my decision, although it seemed that he never really got over it. A couple of years later, when we passed pre-match, he ignored me. I have not spoken with him since.

I knew that, by remaining at Livingston, I would enter a period of uncertainty while the club tried to resolve its financial burdens. Things were evolving at Almondvale and Jim Leishman left Livi to return to his first love, Dunfermline Athletic. When Máximo resigned, he was replaced by the ex-Celtic player and boss Davie Hay. He had been at the club with Leishman from the start and stepped up from his coaching role to take the reins.

Davie Hay (Former Livingston FC Manager) – *Marvin, as a player, was one of the best I have worked with and definitely one of the bravest.*

Under Hay, we were playing decent football and were in the top five by the turn of the year. We were also doing well in the League Cup, knocking out Aberdeen in the quarter-finals after extra time at a cold Pittodrie in December. All the time, though, we knew that the club's financial troubles were deepening. We had heard that they had an overdraft of around £3.5m, which was unfathomable given that we were still regularly attracting 7,000 fans to the stadium and were doing well on the pitch.

We were preparing to play Dundee at Easter Road in the semi-final on 3 February 2004, when we were hit by some shocking news. The club had entered administration that very day. We were all called together and Dominic Keane tearfully delivered the news that the banks had called in their loans. He repeated over and over again the words 'they've failed me, they've failed me' as he came to terms with the fact that he had lost the club. It was now out of his control and the day-to-day running of Livingston Football Club would lie with the administrators.

Despite the devastating news, we maintained our focus on the field and went on to win the Dundee tie 1-0. We had struggled to contend with Dens striker Nacho Novo throughout the game but, with the game still goalless, we were awarded a penalty in the final minute. Again, before Derek Lilley took the penalty, I prayed for God to help us through this hard time. Dee's keeper Julian Speroni was also a Christian, but perhaps my prayer was stronger, because Lilley scored! The win put us into the final of the Scottish League Cup – a great achievement by any standards.

Our opponents in the final at Hampden Park would be Hibernian, who had knocked out Rangers on penalties. Back at Almondvale, the euphoria of coming through the tie did not last long. We immediately experienced the cost-cutting measures that the administrators put into place as soon as they took control. My wages were cut in half and I would be out of contract at the end of the season, with the one-year option torn up. Five other players also had their wages cut while seven were immediately released.

Our preparations for the final were, obviously, not ideal. The released players were given tickets to come along for the occasion, but I am not sure I would have gone considering I was no longer with the club and had been denied the chance to play. More importantly, if they could not find another club, they were out of a job.

We looked forward to the final and it was to be a wonderful day in my life, let alone my career. As I looked around Hampden, all I could see was the green and white of the Hibs fans and a small pocket of Livingston fans in gold. I have an aerial photograph on my wall to this day showing the stadium with that split of colours and fans. They had brought around four times the number of fans we could muster.

Besides being a unique occasion for the club, it was the first major final for all the players. Having put out both Rangers and Celtic, Hibernian were favourites. If they had won, they would have been the first team to put out both halves of the Old Firm and go on to win the trophy. We obviously did not go into the match in the best spirit because of all the off-field problems, but we had already beaten Hibs twice that season and it would all be about who performed on the day. The Hibs side included a number of players who would go on to have a good career, including Kevin Thomson, Scott Brown, Gary Caldwell, Garry O'Connor and Derek Riordan.

When the match kicked off, Hibs came flying at us from the first whistle and they dominated the proceedings in the first half. We were up against it and I had to clear the ball off the line as we struggled to get into the game. Our boys were nervous, especially in the opening moments, and we were not showing what we were capable of. I wondered if the occasion was too much for them. We did not show anything like the quality that had taken us to the final. Our players were tentative against this spirited young Hibs team, but we held things together in the first half and were happy to go in at 0-0. Manager Davie Hay rallied the team at the interval and reminded us that we were still in the game. His message was that we should go out and express ourselves. The nerves had gone by that time and we realised that this was a chance we should truly grasp. We went out for the second half with a new spirit and a positive frame of mind. Right from the kick-off, we began to impose ourselves on the match.

Five minutes after the break, we got the vital opening goal. Burton O'Brien caught the ball just before it drifted out of play on the left and pulled it back for Derek Lilley to sweep the ball into the net. The emotion was palpable as the team enjoyed a surge of confidence, especially when we added the second two minutes later. Jamie McAllister timed his run perfectly to get on the end of a long ball and raced clear. He then slipped the ball neatly past Hibs keeper Daniel Andersson to send our fans into delirium. When the ball went in for that goal, I was asking myself: 'This is so good – is it really happening?' I looked to the sky and thanked the Lord, saying to myself: 'God is good!' What a turnaround it had been.

With a 2-0 lead, we comfortably saw out the match and, at the final whistle, I sank to my knees with tears flowing from my eyes. I took off my shirt to reveal a T-shirt with the following words imprinted boldly on the front: 'With God Nothing is Impossible – Luke 1:37.'

It was a message that seemed particularly apt given the problems the club had experienced in the weeks leading up to the game.

It was a wonderful result for the club, the town and, of course, me personally, but it had come amidst a period of great tragedy for all who had been involved at Livingston. There was huge joy when we were presented with the cup, but also sadness that so many of my team-mates had left and would leave. It should have felt like a new beginning, but in many ways it felt like the end.

It was certainly bittersweet for the fans, who had to balance the joy of winning the cup with the prospect of seeing their club go under. It was no flash in the pan, because we were also doing well in the Scottish Cup and, only a few days later, we beat Aberdeen to set up a semi-final tie with Celtic. We were exhausted for that game – physically and mentally. I had to pass a late fitness test after sustaining an ankle injury in the League Cup Final. It was a really gutsy performance, but we lost out 3-1 to the Celts. The run in both cups, including television revenues, had put around £500,000 into the coffers of the club, but it was a paltry sum compared to the level of debt.

The uncertainty over my own future continued and there had been talk of me going to Rangers. It had continued for several months, but I did not see any substance to it. As far as I was concerned, it was simply rumour. Davie Hay's assistant, Allan Preston, talked up a move, saying: 'Marvin is the best at what he does in Scotland and I include Bobo Balde [Celtic] in that. Don't ask him to hit a 60-yard pass on to the toes of team-mate David Fernandez, but if you want the ball won in the air or on the ground, then he'll do it for you. He's a fantastic player and captain of his country. He's got faults, but his attitude is spot on. He's very fair and there's not a malicious bone in his body and other managers always mention him after we play them. I'm not trying to tell other clubs how to pick their team, but if you see Rangers are without Moore and Khizanishvili, well maybe they need a stopper like Marvin.'

He went on to say that he would not be surprised if I was the subject of interest from other clubs, stressing that, although the club did not want to lose me, they needed the money. He said: 'He's just 28 and he's got the best days of his playing career just ahead of him.' They were nice, complimentary words possibly motivated by the desire to increase my marketability. A move at a decent transfer fee would certainly be good for Livingston, but it could also be best for me.

Besides its financial worries, the club knew that I wanted to play at a higher level. Liverpool had been the club I supported as a boy, simply because I only really knew English football. Playing in Scotland and against both Celtic and Rangers, I now realised that there were big clubs outside the English Premier League. I would have loved a move to either of these clubs, but the idea of possibly moving to Ibrox really thrilled me. It was all paper talk, however, and nothing concrete seemed to develop to indicate that the club were truly interested. Then, out of the blue, I got a phone call from Barry Ferguson's agent, John Viola. I did not know him at the time, but after he told me who he was, he verified that Rangers were indeed interested in signing me. He said that if I wanted it to happen, it could, if I left it to him.

I did not have an agent, so I put matters in the hands of Viola to see what would materialise. A few weeks later, things had moved forward to the stage where I was invited to Rangers owner David Murray's office. A pre-contract agreement was set up with around five games to go in the season. At that stage, I had not even met manager Alex McLeish again, although I still had good memories of the time when he welcomed me to Motherwell as a raw youngster from Trinidad and Tobago. All the negotiations were conducted between Viola and Murray. I found Murray pleasant and impressive, mainly because he was representing Rangers. The pre-contract agreement was put in place and I would sign a three-year deal at the end of the season in May 2004.

When I told my family about my move to Rangers, everyone was delighted for me. I still had to finish off the season with Livingston, but I was already thinking about life at Ibrox. When I played my last game at Almondvale, it was an emotional experience. We beat Hibernian 4-1, which was incidental to my memories of the day. They had figured in the best moment in my football career when we won the League Cup and now they were guests as I parted ways with Livingston.

Alex McLeish (Former manager at Motherwell FC and Rangers FC) – *After winning the treble in 2002/03 the pool was weakened as we lost a lot of top-quality players. The next season was disappointing, and owner David Murray confessed it had left me with a poor deck of cards, compared to the quality I once had available. We sat down to plan out our strategy for the following season, identifying good players who could make a difference without blowing our finances. Around that time, we got our eye on Dado Prso who was quality and I watched him batter the Real Madrid defenders with his physicality. We also saw Jean-Alain Boumsong and did well to get him and Prso on free transfers. We had always wanted good Scots-based players and the likes of Steven Thomson and Kris Boyd had done well for us as great penalty-box goalscorers. This time we also had to look at the defence. Celtic had a big presence in their forward line with Sutton and Hartson and we felt we* *needed strength and height in the centre of the defence. We felt we were being bullied in too many games with the previous squad and needed presence in the squad. Marvin's name came up in the conversations and, of course, I had watched him progress with Livingston. We watched videos of him showing him make vital challenges and some last-ditched tackles. It was a pretty easy decision to go for him and he did not let me down.*

It's true that there were some raised eyebrows when we signed him and Marvin would not fit naturally into the group of some of the Rangers legends who played with the club, but he was accepted by his fellow players immediately and loved by everyone. They could see that he would run through a brick wall for them and he did a great job for me. He can be very proud of what he did for Rangers Football Club.

At the end of the match, I took a lap of honour to wave and to acknowledge the 5,000 fans who waited behind to say their farewells to me. Nobody left the stadium until I had gone inside. I was taken by the warmth displayed by all of the fans. I had seen similar things with other players elsewhere, but I was completely overcome with the thought that there were people standing to honour me. It had been my dream to be held in such esteem by the fans and now was the reality of it all. I had formed a special bond with them and together we had experienced the real highs of promotion and then the cup success, but always in the background was the anxiety of the financial position.

I would move on from a club that still has a place in my heart. From now, however, my eyes would be cast westwards to Glasgow and Rangers. It was a wonderful step in my career and I could not wait to get out there and pull on that famous blue jersey. At last, I would play for a really top club. The coming season would be a huge one for me. Apart from trying to make an impact at Ibrox, I had another dream to fulfil – to help Trinidad and Tobago reach the World Cup finals. A week after that farewell at Almondvale, I would play at Easter Road on 30 May 2004 in an international friendly for my country in a match against my adopted homeland of Scotland. We would lose 4-1, but it was a good run-out on a road we hoped would take us to the finals, which would be hosted by Germany in 2006. There was a lot to look forward to as I left Livingston behind.

Chapter Six

Finally, a Blue Heaven

EARLY IN July 2004, I received a letter from Rangers Football Club telling me to come to their training centre, Murray Park, for pre-season training. On the scheduled date, I left Kirkcaldy for the 90-minute drive that I would make just about every day for the next two years. The club offered me a luxury home not far from the training ground, but I was involved with the church and enjoyed living in Kirkcaldy. They had not asked me to move closer to Glasgow and I was comfortable with the journey each day, so that would be the routine journey I would make every day I was with Rangers.

When I arrived at Murray Park for that first time, the great blue electronic security gates with the club's crest opened as I drove up to them. It was more like some Hollywood residence than a football training ground. The gateman told me to drive around the building to the pro entrance at the rear, where I was directed to meet Jimmy Bell, the club's kit man. I knew all about him from his Livi equivalent Danny Cunning. Although Danny was a Celtic fan, he and Jimmy were great pals and he spoke very highly of the Ranger. Since I had heard so much about him, I was looking forward to our meeting. He did not disappoint.

Jimmy gave me some kit and showed me the assigned place I would have in the dressing room, telling me where to put my gear at the end of training. He showed me around the place and its facilities and I was flabbergasted by it all. At Raith, I had trained in the public park. This was miles better than anything I had seen or experienced before and it certainly lived up to all that I had heard. Although I had never been to the training ground before, everyone in Scottish football had talked about the place and how it was state-of-the-art.

I had been told to arrive at 9.45am for a 10.30am start, but I was actually a little early. Now, that was quite unusual for someone from the Caribbean! I did not want to be late for my first day at this new school! Players Maurice Ross and Bob Malcolm were already there. Both had come through the youth system and graduated to the first-team squad. The others then gradually arrived and everyone was inside the dressing room in good time for training.

Manager Alex McLeish had seen his first-team squad decimated during the summer, with many great players leaving as the club carried out some quite radical cost-cutting. Among those to leave were brothers Frank and Ronald de Boer, Michael Mols, Christian Nerlinger,

Nuno Capucho and Henning Berg. They were all quality players, so there was real pressure on McLeish to win some silverware, as always, while restricted financially over who he could bring in to replace them.

That morning, I was joined by others who had just signed for the club. Rangers – and McLeish in particular – had worked hard to replace those who had left with decent players secured at minimal cost. They included Dado Prso, who had been signed on a free transfer from Monaco, Jean-Alain Boumsong, a free from Auxerre, Nacho Novo, who had come from Dundee for £450,000, and Alex Rae, who was a free transfer from Wolverhampton Wanderers. Shortly afterwards, we were joined by Gregory Vignal, who had come initially on a year-long loan from Liverpool. Mikel Arteta was also there and went through that first training session with me, but the next day he was on his way out of the club on a transfer to Real Sociedad. He was a nice guy, but obviously I would not get the chance to play with him.

The atmosphere among the player group was brilliant from that very first day. Everyone was excited for the new season. Dado Prso was a really funny guy and adapted immediately to his new environment. Shota Arveladze, who had joined the club three years earlier, created a lot of the fun in the dressing room. Then there was Fernando Ricksen – a madman who was up to all sorts of antics, but whom I would find to be an enormously dedicated trainer. He was really unbelievable in training. One of the routines we call 'toro', or 'two-touch', places someone in the middle while the players form a circle, passing the ball around. The player in the middle can't leave until he manages to get the ball. Fernando was rarely in the middle for longer than ten seconds! It was that tenacity to win the ball that would characterise his career.

I would get to know all the players well over the next few days and what a fine bunch they were. Firstly, however, we had our initial training session out on the field with McLeish's assistant, Andy Watson. It was tough! We did a bit of jogging and stretching before getting into the hard running and football. It was that year that the club started rigging the players up with heart monitors to check our fitness levels. It seemed that Watson was pushing us to the limits.

McLeish stood on the sidelines watching us go through the motions and then we played a game, with the manager looking on. I had a misplaced pass and he called to me: 'Marvin, you're not at Livingston any more.' I was taken aback, but that single comment had a huge effect on me. If there had been any doubt, I realised that now I was at a different level and I would have to maintain concentration in everything I did. It was unacceptable to give the ball away cheaply. At Rangers, there would be no room for error and I would have to step up to the mark.

It was a key moment and made a huge impression on me. It altered my approach to the game – life even – at

Ibrox. I realised that there were standards that had to be attained if I was going to be successful here.

Alex McLeish (Manager at Motherwell FC and Rangers FC) – *It is interesting that Marvin should have found that single comment about no longer being at Livingston so important to him. I recall when I was first capped for Scotland I was very nervous in the lead-up, especially since manager Jock Stein had not said anything to me right up until the day of the game. I expected him to tell me what he wanted me to do, but just before that game, he simply said, 'Do what you do for your club.' It completely relaxed me and it was like a eureka moment that I passed on to every central defender that played for me thereafter. I spoke with Marvin and I did not want him to think he had to change his game and start firing world-class passes around the field, like Franck Sauzée. I wanted him to keep things simple and do what he did best, which was defend and make simple passes.*

I would also learn that life was pressurised at Ibrox, because you had to win every game. That was what was expected and I had to gear my mentality to that. At Rangers, you need to be of a certain character to survive. If you do not have that character, then you will not succeed. We have been fortunate along the way to have some of the old-school characters coach the youngsters.

When I was there, John Brown used to bark at the kids, but he was working to instil that winning mentality within them. They paid attention to him, knowing that nothing but the best was expected of them. It was the Rangers way.

When I joined the club, they handed me a little booklet and a DVD which explained what the club was all about – its history and what was expected of Rangers players. It was a nice touch, but it also left me in no doubt that there were high expectations at this club.

Barry Ferguson (Team-mate at Rangers FC) – *When I first read that Marvin was coming to Rangers, I thought it wasn't the best signing, but I think he proved everybody wrong!*

As we played on that first day of training, I was conscious that everyone would be watching and assessing me. It was normal at football clubs for the players to look at new signings and try to suss them out. No matter their background, every new player was under that scrutiny. At the end of the day, I was happy with my performance and drove back up the road to Kirkcaldy delighted to get that first session out of the way. There was no dietician at Ibrox at that time, so I had a couple of yum-yums from the kitchen before I left. I really liked them. After all the calories I had burned in training, I needed them. After a couple of weeks' hard training at Murray Park, we went off to Austria to continue our pre-season preparations. We would play two games there against local side SC Furstenfeld and Italian Serie A side Roma, who were also based in the country for training. The first match would be against the Austrians at their Sportplatz Furstenfeld ground, which had a capacity of 2,500 spectators.

The game was played on 19 July 2004 and I would make my debut in a Rangers jersey. I took my place in the centre of the defence alongside the Georgian, Zurab Khizanishvili. He had signed for the club from Dundee a year earlier and played at centre-back for most of the previous season. Jean-Alain Boumsong would replace Zurab in the next game as my back-four partner. The team had been criticised for being too lightweight in the centre of the defence before our arrival. Celtic had a formidable and physical front-line pairing of John Hartson and Chris Sutton and I think Alex McLeish felt he had to counter that with the physical presence I could bring.

Besides Boumsong, Khizanishvili and myself, Rangers also had Craig Moore as a contender for a central defensive position, but he was unavailable in the early part of the season. He had committed himself to the Australian team for the 2004 Olympics, much to the disappointment of the management. As a result, he had also been stripped of the captaincy by McLeish and the armband had been handed to our German goalkeeper, Stefan Klos. The writing was on the wall for Craig and it was common knowledge that he would leave the club quite soon. He would eventually be moved on in January 2005.

Klos was perhaps not the most obvious choice for the captaincy, because he was a quiet man and clearly played as the last line in the team. He was not the kind who did a lot of shouting, but he had some gravitas as a player who had achieved everything in the game. By the time I came to the club, he had already won three league titles, four Scottish Cups and two League Cups, as well as the domestic treble with Rangers. He had also won the title with his hometown club, Borussia Dortmund, and helped them win the Champions League. If Klos was not the most vocal in the team, I would find that there were many others keen to take the lead.

After settling into the club, I had been desperate for that first chance to wear a blue jersey and it was a great experience. We won 4-0 against the Austrians, with Nacho scoring two of the goals on his debut and Ross McCormack and Peter Lovenkrands getting the others. I felt I played well and had comfortably settled into the side. In the second match against Roma, we won 4-1, with Nacho again scoring twice before Dado Prso added a penalty and Alex Rae completed the scoring. Prso and Rae's goals were also on their debut, so it was a bright start for the new players and things were looking up. Again, I had a comfortable afternoon alongside Boumsong. I could see he was skilful and, although he occasionally took chances with flicks over strikers, there was no doubt that he was class.

When we returned to the UK, there was a friendly with Fulham at Craven Cottage, which we won 1-0, although I did not appear. A few days later, however, I made my Ibrox debut against Tottenham Hotspur in front of 36,000 fans. I was paired again with Boumsong and the back four was completed by Fernando Ricksen on the right and Paolo Vanoli on the left. In the Spurs team, in direct opposition to us, were Robbie Keane and Jermain Defoe. The latter would, amazingly, move to Ibrox 15 years later. Pedro Mendes, another who would become a Ranger, was also in their team that day.

Prior to the match I was really nervous. I prayed, repeating to myself over and over again: 'Do it at your best or not at all.' This was the mantra my grandmother had always instilled in us and it seemed particularly important that day in front of this Ibrox crowd. I gave 100 per cent as I always did and especially in the tackle. When Robbie Keane got on the ball in the first half, I slid in to make a block tackle as he prepared to shoot. I succeeded in clearing the ball but left him crumpled on the field, which seemed to delight the Rangers fans! He had made some statements before the game, saying how much he would love to play for Celtic. The Rangers fans were not happy with that and they let him know. He was taken off and, if I was sorry to see him leave the field with an injury, it did not do my reputation any harm with our fans. They seemed to revel in my commitment and I had left a mark with them.

We went on to beat Spurs 2-0 with goals from Nacho Novo and Dado Prso. It was a perfect start for them in front of the Ibrox fans, but also for me. Besides the enthusiasm that I showed in the game, I was working constantly in training to improve my touch. I was never afraid of hard work and I realised that I had a great opportunity at Rangers. I would continue to work away at my game, also getting some valuable guidance from Alex McLeish. He had been a top-quality defender with Aberdeen and Scotland and obviously knew the position in the centre of the defence.

I explained (in Chapter One) how that first season at Ibrox was to end with that momentous championship win on what is called Helicopter Sunday. It impacted the lives of many and it was one of the happiest moments in my career when we realised we had snatched the title from Celtic. However, the season did not begin nearly as happily as it ended. I had been given the chance to show what I could do, but my Ibrox career would be slow in getting off the ground, partly because of my international commitments. These continued through the latter part of the summer and into the New Year. They were World Cup qualifiers in the main, although there were also Caribbean Cup ties to be played. It was also clear that McLeish had not settled on his preferred back four.

I felt I had done well in the pre-season games, so I was disappointed to be left out of the first couple of competitive matches in the season – against Aberdeen at Pittodrie then CSKA Moscow away in the European Cup third qualifying round. A disappointing draw against the Dons was followed by a 2-1 defeat in the first leg of the European match. It seemed that the manager's preferred central defensive partnership was shaping up to be Jean-Alain Boumsong alongside Zurab Khizanishvili, with Gregory Vignal replacing Paolo Vanoli at right-back.

After the defeat in Moscow, I was drafted in to play alongside Boumsong for our next match. It would be my first competitive game for Rangers and, coincidentally, it would be against my old club, Livingston, at Ibrox. They had enjoyed a good start to the championship, winning their opening match, which put them above us in the league table. It was a fierce game, with no quarter asked or given by both sides, but Rangers emerged comfortable 4-0 winners. It was a strange experience for me because the Livi fans cheered me at the end as I left the field and I returned the compliment by applauding them.

I had moved on, though, and Ibrox was now my home. After the Livi match, I headed back to the Caribbean for a World Cup qualifier against Saint Vincent and Grenadines. Rangers had no control when Trinidad and Tobago called for my release. I was, of course, delighted to play for my country, although I realised that the hectic qualifying schedule could disrupt my appearances for Rangers in the early part of the 2004/05 season at least.

Zurab came back in to replace me in the next match and when I returned, Craig Moore, whom we called 'Oz' due to his Aussie background, slotted into the position for the return leg of the CSKA match at Ibrox. I had to be content with a place on the bench. We needed a win and, with the game sitting at 1-1, I was thrown on as a makeshift striker in a final throw of the dice. The goal never came and we went out of the competition, losing a potential windfall of £8m in the process. It was disappointing that I had only played a minor part in the tie, but I guess that the manager wanted the European experience of 'Oz', even though his future seemed destined to be away from Ibrox.

Moore retained his place for the next match just four days later, which was the opening league encounter with Old Firm rivals Celtic at Parkhead. It gave me a chance to see the atmosphere at first-hand, although a late goal by Alan Thompson gave them the points. We had lost the last seven games against Celtic and, although I was new to the club, I understood that was unacceptable, particularly to the fans. The result put McLeish under pressure and it was compounded when we followed up the Old Firm defeat with a disappointing 0-0 draw at Tynecastle and a 1-0 defeat to CS Maritimo in the first leg of our UEFA Cup first-round tie. The draw against Hearts left us seven points behind leaders Celtic with just five games played. I had played just that solitary game against Livingston.

I was on the fringes of the team and apparently still not favoured. It seemed that the manager's preferred central defensive partnership was now 'Oz and Boumsong, so I would just have to keep working away until the chance came to get back into the side. After two more league games without being chosen, an opportunity at last came for me to get back into the side. Injury ruled Moore out of the league match against Dundee at Dens Park, so I got a recall and played well in a 2-0 win. My return to the side was short-lived. Even though I had done all that was asked of me, I was left out for the return leg against CS Maritimo as Zurab came back into the team. We won the tie on penalties after matching their first-leg 1-0 result.

I was recalled for the next match after that European tie, which would be the last before the international break. A pleasing 2-0 win over Kilmarnock at Ibrox on 3 October 2004 was the perfect lift for me heading off to the Caribbean, especially since I scored my first goal for Rangers. It was a special day for me. Ironically, the team had not lost a goal in the two competitive matches I played up to the end of September. That match against Killie gave me the chance of a run in the side through October, as we then went on to beat Motherwell and then Amica Wronki in the UEFA Cup. That had produced three straight victories without the loss of a goal and things began to tilt in my favour.

Maybe I was being seen to be answering the doubts that many shared over whether I could be a Rangers player. It was something I was always conscious of, but I had been determined to show my worth when I got the chance. The run would continue as the manager settled on playing me alongside Boumsong at the heart of his defence. I built a good understanding with the Frenchman and we started to hit a good run of form. I had fulfilled my dream of playing for a top team and that match against Kilmarnock was something of a turning point. People had said that I would just be a fringe player, but I was proving them wrong. I did not join Rangers to simply be a squad player. I had signed to do a job for them and I was determined to get into the team and stay in it.

As we started to blend better as a side, all eyes were on a League Cup quarter-final tie against Celtic at Ibrox in November 2004. In the run-up to that match, we played seven matches after my introduction to the side, drawing just once, while also continuing our progress in the UEFA Cup. We were also scoring, too, with 21 goals for and just three conceded. Our confidence was high and I was desperate to be involved after missing out on the club's previous visit to Celtic Park.

It seemed that everyone was relishing the tie and there was an added burden on the manager. He had to stop the run of victories Celtic had built up and there was also the possibility of a trophy at stake. The newspapers focused on the physical clash there would be between me and John Hartson. He was not the quickest on the ground, but he was the type of player who could bully a defender if they were not able to stand up to him. It was not all about Hartson, though. He would be paired with the Brazilian, Juninho, who was tricky and could be a handful.

We were up for the match and I was ready. Coming out on to the field, the noise inside our stadium was incredible as the fans exchanged their songs. As usual, I was nervous, but very much focused. I settled into the frantic pace immediately and found that not only would I have to deal with Hartson, but also Juninho. He was cleverly singling me out, trying to create space by drawing me out of the defence. I knew what his plan was, so I allowed him to retreat and I stayed firmly in our defensive shape. Celtic were not committing a lot of men forward, so Juninho's impact was nullified if Jean-Alain and I could keep things tight.

The game was level at half-time but Celtic got the breakthrough early in the second half when, following a free kick, Hartson stole a yard and got a run on me as the ball came into the box, heading past Klos. It knocked our confidence a bit, especially when they went through a phase of possession with their fans shouting 'Olé' at every touch. We were not beaten, though, and began to put them under intense pressure. Shota Arveladze came on for Lovenkrands to freshen things up and, with just five minutes to go, he picked up a loose pass from Thompson.

He played the ball out to Nacho and when Celtic keeper Marshall beat out his shot to Dado Prso, he pounced on the rebound. As he rolled the ball into the net, the celebrations inside Ibrox erupted. What joy!

We could have grabbed a winner late in normal time when I almost got on the end of a loose ball. When the game went into extra time, we had the momentum, piling on the pressure. Then, with just nine minutes left, Arveladze got on the end of a break to send a shot into the corner of the net. There would be no more scoring. When the referee blew the final whistle, confirming our victory, the relief inside Ibrox was huge. I enjoyed every minute of it – the tension, the excitement, the atmosphere and the fans, who were deliriously happy. It was a fantastic game and I knew that I had achieved something special in playing for Rangers. To play in that fixture alone is wonderful, but to emerge as victors in these circumstances was just fantastic. I think we all sensed that this match was a turning point for us.

We would face Celtic again ten days later in the league, but next up would be Hibs at Easter Road. Things almost came off the rails when Nacho received a red card after 28 minutes. Thankfully, Dado snatched the only goal from the penalty spot, but our concern was that Nacho would be suspended for the Old Firm match. He had been such an important player for us in the cup tie. Thankfully, the card was downgraded to a yellow, so he was available.

What a match that next Celtic game was to turn out to be. Nacho Novo gave us the lead from the penalty spot on 15 minutes after he had been upended in the box. Then, about 20 minutes later, Dado Prso got his heavily bandaged head to the ball to score the second from around eight yards. In the second half, the match deteriorated, with many of the Celtic players losing their discipline. Alan Thompson head-butted Peter Lovenkrands and was shown a red card, then Chris Sutton was also sent off for two yellow cards. They finished the game with nine men and we comfortably saw a out the match to win 2-0.

If things were going well in the championship, we fared less favourably in Europe. We went out of the UEFA Cup after losing our final group game against Auxerre 2-0 at Ibrox when a draw would have taken us through. Graeme Souness was manager of Newcastle United and he had made enquiries about Boumsong, who had enjoyed a good start to his Ibrox career. With no lucrative European football after December for Rangers, the club decided to part with him in January for £8.5m. The club would lose a good player but needed the cash injection. Boumsong's dream move to Newcastle did not turn out so well and I was not so surprised. He was a great player, but he was inclined to take chances, like flicking the ball over the heads of attackers. He would not get away with that for long in the FA Premier League, but he was a great player nonetheless and I was sorry to see him leave.

Just three weeks after the disappointment of our European exit, we went out of the Scottish Cup to Celtic in the third round, losing 2-1 at Parkhead. Zurab was my partner that day, but Rangers were actively working on a replacement for Boumsong. They brought in 25-year-old Sotirios Kyrgiakos from Panathinaikos at a fee of £1.7m. What a signing he turned out to be. He was excellent in the air and fierce in the tackle – a real battler. It had been a mixed start to the season for me, but latterly I had secured my position in the side. Our defence looked formidable and I enjoyed playing alongside Kyrgiakos. It took some time for the team to gel, but the team became more balanced as the season progressed.

Although we had suffered setbacks against Auxerre and Celtic, the team actually went on a long unbeaten run in the league from December 2004. By the end of February 2005, we were six points ahead in the championship, although our Old Firm rivals had two games in hand. Our advantage was courtesy of a magnificent win at Celtic Park on 20 February 2005 when two goals in the last 20 minutes from Gregory Vignal and Nacho Novo gave us the points. Our goalkeeper that day was Ronald Waterreus, as Stefan Klos had suffered a bad knee injury a few weeks earlier. Ironically, the injury he sustained was identical to the ACL that I was to suffer. Waterreus handled everything Celtic could throw at him as we tried to quell the threat of Craig Bellamy, who had arrived at Celtic just a week earlier. It put an end to their 11-

From that same play-off match, Salman Isa is tackled by me and Kelvin Jack

Bank of Scotland Premier Division, Celtic v Rangers, Celtic Park. I clear from John Hartson

Celtic's John Hartson and Bobo Balde jump for the ball with Rangers' Sotirios Kyrgiakos and me during the Bank o fScotland Premier League match at Ibrox on Sunday, 12 February 2006

Bank of Scotland Premier Division, Rangers v Heart of Midlothian at Ibrox Stadium. I am celebrating scoring

Coming out on top against Neil Lennon

Coming out of the tunnel at Easter Road after our historic win on 'Helicopter Sunday'

My message displayed by the fans – 'Keep Believing'

Nacho Novo and me celebrate with the championship trophy

Celebrating winning the Irn-Bru SFL Second Division title with Raith Rovers after the crucial match v Arbroath on 9 May 2009 at Starks Park, Kirkcaldy

Challenging Rangers' Andy Little while with Forfar Athletic during our Scottish Communities League Cup, first round match at Station Park, Forfar

Former Livingston boss, Jim Leishman and me

Singing with Scottish singer-songwriter Callum Beattie at the Rangers fanzone

At Ibrox in my Rangers hospitality role in October 2019

game unbeaten run at home in the derby and was clearly a vital result. It was also pleasurable to get revenge for our Scottish Cup disappointment at the hands of the Celts.

Things were shaping up well in the league after our poor start and we were still in the last four of the League Cup. Our focus remained on the title race and the Old Firm result should have pushed us on, but a shock last-minute goal conceded against Inverness Caley Thistle at Ibrox two weeks later swiftly killed our advantage. If Celtic won their three games in hand they would have the lead in the championship race. A week later and it looked like that last-minute injury at Dundee would end my season. As I explained earlier, that ACL injury was to become part of the drama that would unfold in the run-up to Helicopter Sunday.

I was in the side playing in my usual central defensive position and, I felt, performing solidly. There was a lot of pressure on us, as Rangers were always expected to win every game and this expectation was even greater because things were so tight at the top of the table. We were virtually neck-and-neck with our great rivals, Celtic, so the need to get a win and three points became particularly important.

It had been a pretty dismal game and was goalless, but it came to life inside the last ten minutes. As we pushed for that opening, we got a corner which Dutch star Fernando Ricksen delivered deep into the box. I lunged at it, getting my head firmly to the ball six yards out to score what would prove to be a vital goal. Fernando added a second two minutes later and we closed out the game for a 2-0 victory. The win continued our unbeaten run of 26 games league games and kept us four points ahead of Celtic at the top, although they had two games in hand. If they won these, they would lead us by two points. There were now only eight games left and it was going to be tight.

From then, I would look on, desperate to get back into the action, and by mid-April we had faltered further, losing 1-0 to Dundee United at Ibrox. It was our first defeat in the league in 28 matches. That left us five points behind with a game in hand. It was nip and tuck, but time was now running out. Throughout this period, I was working my way back to fitness, as I have already explained, placing my faith in God that I would be healed. That faith would reward me with the jersey once again as we faced Celtic at Ibrox with five games to go. If I had joy at returning to play once more, there was disappointment in the 2-1 defeat we suffered at the hands of our rivals. It looked like the title would escape us until that dramatic day at Easter Road when the helicopter changed direction. It had been a season of resilience in the face of many disappointments. The rest, as they say, is history.

Perhaps the upsets through the season prepared us for that final push. It just needed that little bit of faith to get us over the line and how more dramatic could it have been? I did not falter in my belief that we would get there.

I had won my first piece of silverware with Rangers in historic fashion. Celtic were hurt badly and we knew that they would come back at us next time out.

It had certainly been an eventful season and it finished quite emotionally for me when I was voted the Players' Player of the Year at Rangers. This was a huge honour for someone who had started at the club amidst doubts over whether I was good enough for Rangers. To then discover that my team-mates had voted me their Player of the Year was very moving. When I went up to collect the award in front of fans and staff at a special night at a Glasgow hotel, my team-mates and the assembled guests gave me a standing ovation, which was touching. To emerge from a group of such great players that season including Barry Ferguson, Fernando Ricksen, Dado Prso and Nacho Novo was wonderful. It was a fine way to finish my first year as a Rangers player.

As the season closed in Scotland, my eyes turned once again to the qualifying matches for the World Cup. It would be a busy summer for me and then we would go once again for more Rangers success. What would the 2005/06 season hold?

Well, it certainly did not have the drama of 2004/05, as our performances dipped. World Cup duty prevented me from taking part in most of the pre-season matches, including the club's trip to Canada. I did return at the end of July for a friendly against St Mirren at Love Street, which we won 1-0. Again, there had been an overhaul of the squad, with the likes of Shota Arveladze and Michael Ball leaving and an influx of new players, including Ian Murray from Hibs, José-Karl Pierre-Fanfan from Paris Saint-Germain and Brahim Hemdani from Marseilles. Former Everton star Francis Jeffers was another who came in on a loan, from Charlton Athletic. The new arrivals did not stimulate better performances from the team and Helicopter Sunday soon became a distant memory.

It had all started brightly enough and we negotiated a potentially tricky European Cup tie against Cypriot side Anorthosis. Meanwhile, I was starting to find my place threatened by the introduction of Julian Rodriguez, a £1m acquisition from Monaco. He formed the central defensive partnership with Sotirios Kyrgiakos and I found my appearances increasingly limited.

By the beginning of November 2005, a poor goalless draw with Aberdeen at Ibrox left us in fourth place in the table, 12 points behind surprise leaders Hearts. Celtic had a game in hand that could take them level with the Edinburgh side, so we were languishing in unfamiliar territory after just 14 league games. I had appeared in the starting XI in half of these games. In one of my appearances, we had beaten Celtic 3-1 in our opening league encounter with them. We had not lost in any of the other games I had featured in, but it appeared that manager Alex McLeish had not settled on his preferred defensive partnership.

In November, things deteriorated further. We lost 2-0 to Celtic at Parkhead in the Scottish League Cup quarter-finals and then, just ten days later, we lost again away to our rivals, this time 3-0 in the league. I had managed to regain my place in the side by then. The pressure was immense on the manager. Chairman David Murray had stepped in to call for more fight from the squad and also told McLeish that he had until the end of the month to sort things out. It was looking bleak for him but, with the league looking virtually out of reach, we still had momentum in the European Cup. That competition was our only respite in what was shaping up to be an otherwise forgettable campaign.

The one shining light that changed much of our fortune as we went into 2006 was Kris Boyd, the young Kilmarnock striker who joined in late December 2005. He had already scored against us earlier in the season and was the top goalscorer in the SPL with 15 goals from 19 appearances. At £400,000, the investment looked a great one. The 22-year-old had a huge amount of promise and provided some optimism going forward. He was a remarkable young talent who went on to make a wonderful start for us. He scored a hat-trick on his debut in a 5-0 Scottish Cup third-round win over Peterhead at Ibrox and went on to score seven goals in his first four starts for the club. He would end up with 20 goals for Rangers that season and finished top goalscorer in the SPL with 37 goals. His signing certainly kicked us on somewhat, but even his goals could not salvage the league campaign.

As the year drew to a close, the club went through the worst run in its history. Ten games without a win was well short of where the club needed to be. Although we came back with six straight victories, a 3-0 defeat in the Scottish Cup fourth round against Hibernian at Ibrox in February 2006 ended any realistic hope of silverware for the season. The defeat prompted protests outside Ibrox against both manager McLeish and owner Murray. A few days later, Murray, chastened by the reaction, announced that McLeish would leave his position as manager at the end of the season after four and a half years with the club. McLeish was professional to the end, working as hard behind the scenes as he had at any time I had seen.

He had done well with limited financial backing, while also losing some of his best players as the club tried to reduce its wage bill. I had to thank him for giving me the chance at this great club, but there was now an uncertain future for me, too, with plans already afoot for a new manager.

Around that time, there had been speculation that the new manager would be Paul Le Guen from Olympique Lyonnais. It was an open secret that he had been house-hunting in Glasgow and that preliminary discussions, at least, had been taking place. It was hardly ideal preparation for our last Old Firm game, which was played a few days after we followed up our devastating loss to Hibs by losing to Aberdeen at Pittodrie. Within a few weeks, Murray confirmed that Le Guen had signed a three-year deal to become manager at the end of the season. It was a peculiar situation to have Alex McLeish in place, all the time knowing that he would not be there at the end of the season and that his replacement was waiting in the wings.

I had maintained my place in the side and played right up until that Old Firm clash. We lost the match to the only goal from Maciej Zurawski. It was a horrible goal to lose. He latched on to a ball which had been bobbling about outside our area after some misplaced headers. The game left any hopes of recovering in the championship race in tatters. We were 18 points behind Celtic and there was no way back from that.

The Champions League was to be our solace in what was turning out to be a difficult season. We would go on to become the first Scottish team to reach the last 16 in the tournament and, for all the problems we had endured domestically, it was a great achievement. We had emerged from a tough group that had included Inter Milan, Porto and Artmedia Bratislava, finishing as runners-up.

It had been a wonderful achievement for us to venture so far in the competition. We had lost just once in the group stage – against Inter Milan – and had eliminated Porto, who were one of the favourites. Our draw away to Porto was a testament to McLeish, who helped turn things around in the closing stages. Trailing 1-0 down, he decided to introduce the energy of two youngsters – Chris Burke and Ross McCormack. They combined to allow the 19-year-old McCormack the chance to go through and score the vital equaliser for us with just seven minutes left.

After that great result in Portugal, a draw at Ibrox against Inter Milan was all that we needed to qualify, subject to Artmedia not winning in Bratislava against Porto. As it turned out, that game ended 0-0, so our 1-1 draw at Ibrox was enough. That was a huge point for us, because Inter were top of the Serie A at the time and we were still struggling domestically. The Italian club had some wonderful players. These included the forward Adriano, who scored their only goal. I saw at first-hand what he could do when he managed to steal a yard from me at a corner to head past Waterreus from close in. Actually, as the ball came in, he pushed me to create some space for himself.

Then there was Obafemi Martins, their Nigerian forward who had electrifying speed. Everything was orchestrated for them through their captain, Marco Materazzi, who was extremely skilful. Our equaliser came just eight minutes after Adriano's goal, Thomas Buffel putting a slide-rule pass through for Peter Lovenkrands to run on and beat Francesco Toldo in the Inter goal.

Through all of these wonderful moments in our European adventure, the pressure remained on McLeish, but he was stoic. At least both he and the team had a last-16 European match to look forward to. It came ten days after our defeat by Celtic at Ibrox in February 2006. After that Old Firm loss, I would not play for the club again for almost three months, missing the remainder of our European campaign.

Shortly after the disappointment against Celtic, we met Villarreal at Ibrox in that vital Champions League tie. They had some wonderful players in their side. It was a spirited performance from the side after recovering from an early goal from the penalty spot by Juan Román Riquelme. Peter Lovenkrands equalised, then Uruguayan international Diego Forlán scored a second for Villarreal before half-time. We pushed for the equaliser and got it with eight minutes to go when Juan Manuel Peña deflected a cross from Thomas Buffel into his own goal. We should have won it right at the end when a Spanish defender handled inside the box, but the referee waved away our claims.

In the second leg, we needed a win or a high-scoring draw to go through. Lovenkrands gave us hope with the opening goal on 12 minutes, but an equaliser just after half-time was enough to see Villarreal through on away goals. It had been a valiant effort, but our European campaign ended.

With just three matches left in the season, I finally made an appearance as a substitute in a league match against Kilmarnock at Rugby Park. We were down at the interval and, although he was destined to leave,

Alex McLeish was angry with the team's performance. It showed that he retained the passion for the game and the club, despite his impending exit. I came on in the second half for Alan Hutton and scored twice to help us to a 3-1 win. It was special getting that double and it secured a place in the team for the last two games of the season, both of which we won – 2-1 at Easter Road against Hibs then 2-0 at Ibrox against Hearts. The latter would be my final appearance in a Rangers jersey.

By then, Rangers had lost out to the Tynecastle club for second position in the league to miss out on a spot in the second qualifying round for the lucrative Champions League. We had to be content with a UEFA Cup place. At the end of the match, the players and manager waved sad farewells to the fans. Like some of the other players, I knew it would probably be the end of the road for me.

McLeish deserved enormous credit for what he had achieved at Rangers over five seasons during which the club effectively downsized. He had won the domestic treble and also took the club to that historic success on Helicopter Sunday. Two league championships, two Scottish Cups and three League Cups was a remarkable haul in a period of austerity when many good players had to be sacrificed.

All of the players were extremely supportive of the manager and we felt that we had let him down that season. Even though we knew McLeish would leave at the end of the season, we all worked hard to do our best for him. I personally had a lot to thank him for besides his decision to bring me to Ibrox. He had stood by my side to support me when I had been criticised. We had a great relationship, even though he was the first to reject me as a player when I went to Motherwell all those years ago. He was right then, as I was raw, but hopefully I repaid him for the faith he showed in me later.

Right to the end of his tenure, McLeish showed great strength and character, continuing to fight when the season was lost. When he finally left, he walked out with his head held high and I am sure this was recognised and appreciated by the fans. It was well deserved when he walked into the job as manager of Scotland, in which he also did well.

Looking back over that season, it is difficult to fathom why it should have turned out so badly after our success just a year earlier. Much of my reasoning was that, collectively, we did not appreciate what God had done for us. We did not show gratitude and, in these circumstances, how can you go and ask for something else? That is how God is – if he does something for you, you cannot expect him to do it again if you do not show thanks. He gave us a gift with the championship in the unlikeliest of circumstances, but we did not acknowledge that. I was the only one who came out to recognise what he had done for us in giving us the championship. If the people at Ibrox had done the same, I believe that no one could have stopped us that following year.

Paul Le Guen arrived at Ibrox as soon as the season finished. My focus immediately switched to the World Cup as I headed out to join up with my international team-mates. My future after the World Cup would take care of itself. But now, it was all about the Soca Warriors.

When I returned to Murray Park after the World Cup, pre-season training was already under way and Paul Le Guen took me aside to say that I was not in his plans for the future. I would be given a free transfer and I must say that my departure was handled cordially. I was two years into a three-year contract and the club paid me up to the end of it to release me. I respected Le Guen's decision because that is football. Some might like your style, while others do not. I was not the only one who would leave. He had a clear-out including Ronald Waterreus, Peter Lovenkrands, Alex Rae, Sotirios Kyrgiakos, Fernando Ricksen, Hamed Namouchi, Bob Malcolm, José-Karl Pierre-Fanfan, Olivier Bernard and Ross McCormack. Le Guen had access to a lot of money when Rangers signed a deal with JJB Sports, giving him free rein to bring in a lot of new players.

Before I left, I went to see my good mates who were remaining at Ibrox and there was a lot of hugging and exchanging of good wishes. The dressing room had changed, with many new players, but I had final farewell chats with Jimmy Bell, the physios, the cooks and everyone on the ground staff with whom I had built up a good relationship. The kitchen staff arranged some yum-

yums for me, knowing that these were my favourites. I then picked up my gear and left the Rangers training ground for the last time.

I think I surprised many people when I was at Ibrox. Even Alex McLeish conceded some time later that he never thought I would play as many games as I did. He said: 'It's a credit to the form he showed. He kept his game simple. He was a very strong defender and was very rarely beaten in the air. In fact, he was just about unbeatable in the air.'

I had to close the Rangers chapter in my life and think about a new future. Many people had said they regretted me leaving and that they would miss me not being around the club for my fun and chat, which was nice. Just as I had believed that God had guided me to this club, it was God who had decided it was my time to move on. Everything is done to God's plan. Despite that, as a human being, I was sad to leave, as Rangers had given me a special time in my life.

As everyone knows by now, things did not work out well for Paul Le Guen at Ibrox. Barry Ferguson and I were on the phone constantly and I knew that, behind the scenes, things were not going well. However, I was astonished when Le Guen stripped Barry of the captaincy, which I know hurt him deeply, causing a lot of emotional strife. Although I had nothing but respect for how Le Guen handled my departure, I was dismayed at how he dealt with Barry. Le Guen compounded the situation by removing him from the team and stating that he had no place in his future plans for Rangers. Publicly, Murray apparently backed his new manager.

Le Guen clearly knew nothing about the player or the club and I was not surprised by the outrage that followed. In my opinion, Barry is up there with the great players, great captains and great servants for Rangers Football Club. Had he left the club in these circumstances, there would have been mayhem. Thankfully for Barry Ferguson and Rangers, it ended well with the return of Walter Smith as manager and the departure of the Frenchman.

Chapter Seven

The Soca Warriors and a World Cup Dream

TO QUALIFY for the World Cup finals was a dream shared by everyone in Trinidad and Tobago. The disappointments of the qualification campaigns for the 1974 and 1990 tournaments lingered for many, leaving a sour taste in the mouth. It seemed as if failure to qualify would be forever our destiny. However, the prospect of an appearance on that world stage arose once again in the lead-up to the 2006 tournament, scheduled for Germany.

In our previous attempt, for the 2002 finals, everyone had expected we would qualify.

It had all started so well for us in the Caribbean phase of the qualification process with a 5-0 win over Netherlands Antilles on 4 March 2000. I scored the team's opening goal on 19 minutes with a back-post header for what was my first World Cup goal. We then defeated Canada, Mexico and Panama in the semi-final group stage, finishing top of the table and reaching a heady 29th in the FIFA world rankings.

It all started to go wrong in the final phase of six teams, where we were joined by Costa Rica, Honduras, Jamaica, Mexico and the United States. Three would qualify automatically, so we felt we had a great chance. We got off to the worst possible start, though, losing our first two matches, away to Jamaica and Costa Rica. We then salvaged a home draw against Mexico but lost our next two matches, at home to Honduras and away to the United States. Qualification would be difficult now but, with five games to play, we still had a chance.

We had a new coach in Brazilian Rene Simoes and he took the team off on a tour of Bermuda at the end of June 2001 as part of the preparation for a final push to qualify. We would play a vital qualifier against Jamaica immediately on our return. We beat Bermuda 5-0 in a friendly, so we were in good shape. Afterwards, however, Russell Latapy and Dwight Yorke did not turn up for a training session.

Simoes later said: 'He [Yorke] failed to show up for the training session and unfortunately we had to kick him out of the squad. That was a real shame, because he was playing good football for Trinidad's national team and the country was counting on him to take them to their first World Cup. Someone came to me and said that they [Yorke and Latapy] had had a lot to drink and that's why they didn't show up for training. That left me without a choice. I had to kick them out.'

The two players responded by saying that they had quit international football and it 'was in the interests of all concerned'. It was not a good situation, as we had now lost our two top players at a vital time, with our qualification hopes hanging by a thread. From there, our campaign just fell apart. It was heartbreaking. We still had hopes of qualifying, but everything went downhill from there.

We completed the campaign, winning just once, a 1-0 victory in Honduras in the penultimate game, and finished bottom of the group with just five points. Whether the whole affair was a misunderstanding or ill discipline, it had left our hopes in tatters. Costa Rica, Mexico and the United States qualified for Japan and South Korea, and that summer, as I watched the finals, I knew we could have done well in the tournament, but it was not to be. Another chance had gone and the football federation had to get things sorted out in time for us to have another go for the 2006 tournament.

It was clear to me that we had to get Latapy and Yorke back into the squad if we were going to have a decent chance of qualifying. Rene Simoes moved on after a year, so there was no impediment in that regard, but someone had to find a solution.

The quest for the 2006 finals began for us in the summer of 2004 when, along with another 33 CONCACAF teams, we started the long battle to secure just three qualification spots. A fourth place could be available after a play-off between the fourth-placed country and a team from the Asian Football Confederation.

In preparation for the campaign, we played several friendly matches and the last two would be against Scotland and Northern Ireland. These would give the players a chance to test themselves against European opposition in the event that we were successful in qualifying. The Scotland match was played at Easter Road in Edinburgh on 30 May 2004 in front of a crowd of more than 16,000. In our side were a few players, besides myself, who played in the UK. They included Brent Sancho, who was with Dundee, Ian Cox, who was actually English-born and played for Gillingham, Carlos Edwards of Wrexham and Stern John, who had made a name for himself with Nottingham Forest and Birmingham City. Kenwyne Jones had just signed with Southampton, but the rest had played all their careers in Trinidad and Tobago.

We had a miserable first half and were 4-0 down at the break, but Stern John pulled one back in the second half as we started to get a grip on the match. Some of the players who were unfamiliar with the British game found it hard to deal with the pace of the match, but it gave them a taste for professional football in the country. Our next game, played seven days later, was against Northern Ireland and was in more familiar conditions at Tobago's

Dwight Yorke Stadium in Bacolet. Again, we slid to defeat – this time by 3-0 – but the matches were not so much about the results as getting the players into shape for the World Cup campaign.

The CONCACAF qualifying competition would begin for us a week later, beginning with a second-round tie against Dominican Republic, after receiving a bye in the first round. The match would be played over two legs, with the first held at the Estadio Olimpico Juan, Santo Domingo. After a goalless first half, I managed to score our first goal on the hour and Stern John got the crucial second for a 2-0 win. In the return, back home in Trinidad, we completed the job by winning 4-0, all of the goals coming in the second half.

The process then involved the winning teams going into three groups of four teams, with the top two in each group moving forward into another league phase for the fourth round. Our group included Saint Kitts and Nevis, Mexico and Saint Vincent and Grenadines, with the matches to be played between August and November 2004. The matches would inevitably conflict with my obligations to Rangers in that first season with the club, but my country would always come first, especially with World Cup qualification at stake.

Mexico were the best team in the group and we lost both matches against them. With two teams to qualify, it was essential we fared much better against the others and, although we needed late goals on more than one occasion, we won all four games to finish a comfortable second in the group. That got us into the crucial fourth-round league phase when the qualification places would be up for grabs. We were joined in the six-team group by Costa Rica, Guatemala, Mexico, Panama and the United States. The top three teams would go to the World Cup finals and there would be a possible additional place via a play-off for the team finishing fourth. The games would kick off in February 2005, by which time I had secured a regular starting place in the Rangers team.

This six-team group phase was known as the 'Hexagonal', or 'Hex' for short. It was where dreams could be fulfilled, but where hopes could also be left in tatters. Indeed, after just three games, that is exactly where we looked to be. We lost our first match 2-1 against the USA at the Queens Park Oval ground at home in Port of Spain. The American team included DaMarcus Beasley, who would go on to play for Rangers.

Unfortunately, that terrible injury I sustained at Dundee on 13 March 2005 came less than two weeks before we were due to meet Guatemala in the second match of the league phase. It was disastrous for the team, as they lost 5-1 away. A goalless draw in the third match, at home to Costa Rica, left our fans in despair as we sat bottom of the table. Injury had prevented me from playing in both matches, but I was desperate to return and help push the team back into form.

The nation's football authorities stepped in to try to reverse the fortunes of the team, sacking manager Bertille St Clair and replacing him with Dutchman Leo Beenhakker. The Trinidad and Tobago Football Federation also made another appointment that was important to the morale of the team and the fans. CONCACAF supremo Jack Warner had a role in convincing Russell Latapy and Dwight Yorke to end their international exile. It was announced that former captain Latapy would be returning, not only as a player, but as assistant coach. His fallout after the last World Cup had been forgotten and the move was a good piece of diplomacy to welcome him back into the fold along with Yorke.

Now we had two great players back at our disposal and a renewed spirit as we began working under an international manager of some renown. Beenhakker's appointment, in particular, was inspired. He had fantastic credentials as a coach, managing the Dutch national side and leading both Ajax and Feyenoord to Dutch championships, as well as achieving success with Real Madrid. He was certainly top drawer and he immediately made an impact on the squad. One of the areas he had to work on was the culture, which mirrored that of the country. We are typically laid-back people and maybe the attitude was not always focused. In the past, if the team lost a match, it was not unusual to see everyone laughing and joking as if defeat was just one of those things. It was completely different from what he had experienced in the past and he changed it all quietly and effectively.

It was interesting how he used the attitudes and cultures that were ingrained in the players to turn them into the type he needed. Timekeeping was always a problem, but it was rarely considered an issue in Trinidad and Tobago, where the people are extremely relaxed about time. Beenhakker managed to get the players to recognise that it was important for them to be professional and to ensure that everyone was there at the start of training and remained until the end.

I was highly impressed with his man-management and, after only a few games, the feedback from the entire squad was positive about him. He had instilled a more professional approach and brought organisation to the team. That really sparked a revival, and the self-belief that had faded after our poor start began to return. He gathered everyone together in May 2005 and, despite some concern from some players about burnout, set up four friendlies in three weeks, probably to see what he had in the squad. That caused some media criticism, but we had no doubt he knew what he was doing.

He was fun to listen to and quite a character, with a cigar seemingly always in his mouth. As he spoke, you could sense the wealth of experience he had gathered. His favourite phrase was 'the wonderful, wild jungle of football' and you could appreciate the wisdom behind everything he said.

If he made some positive changes in the team's approach, his tactical influence was immense. He organised us into a 4-4-1-1 formation and worked to improve our defending. Every player would become a defender when not in possession, keeping the team's shape. Of course, these early changes took place when I was trying to recover from injury but, by the time we played our next World Cup 'Hex' match against Panama, I was back in the defence. A 2-0 win kept our hopes alive, although we went down by the same scoreline to Mexico just four days later. The local press observed, however, that there was more organisation about the team.

By September 2005, things were not looking much brighter for us; a 3-2 victory over Guatemala was sandwiched between defeats by the USA and Costa Rica. It looked like third place would be a shoot-out between Guatemala, Costa Rica and ourselves, as the USA and Mexico looked good for the first two spots. With just two matches left, there was no room for further error. We would need to defeat both Panama and Mexico to have a chance. A Stern John goal got us the win over Panama, but Costa Rica created something of a shock by beating the USA 3-0 to secure third place. Now, everything was on the final game. If we failed to beat Mexico, and Guatemala managed to win against Costa Rica, we would be out. However, a win against the Mexicans would give us that fourth position, keeping our hopes of qualification alive via a play-off.

Hasely Crawford Stadium in Port of Spain was packed with 23,000 fans but the first half did not go quite as we had planned. Stern John missed a penalty, which caused concern all around, and then, on 38 minutes, we were stunned when Mexico scored. We fought back and John made amends for his earlier miss by snatching the equaliser just before half-time. We pushed on in the second half for the vital winner. With just over 20 minutes left, John completed a wonderful turnaround for the team and him personally when he scored a wonderful goal with a stunning left-foot shot. It fairly whistled into the top corner from the edge of the box. The noise inside the stadium was immense, especially at the end when we closed out the match for the 2-1 win. We had successfully put up the shutters, restricting the Mexicans to speculative efforts. It was a fantastic result, especially when we learned that Guatemala did, indeed, beat Costa Rica for the points that would have taken them into that crucial fourth spot if we had slipped up.

The road to Germany 2006 was now open to us if we could defeat Bahrain, who had emerged from the Asian Football Confederation (AFC) qualification process. We would have just four weeks until we played the first of the two legs, with the opening game taking place at home in Port of Spain. It was a huge occasion for both nations, as neither had ever qualified for the World Cup. Once again, we had an almost full stadium, with just under 25,000 eagerly but nervously looking on.

The anxiety of the fans was mirrored by the players on the pitch. Both teams were tentative, as no one wanted to make any mistakes. Then, in the 72nd minute, Bahrain scored. It could easily have sent everyone into panic mode, given what was at stake. There was a sense of horror at the prospect of another failure. However, Chris Birchall calmed the nerves somewhat by getting the equaliser and what a goal it was! The ball deflected towards him off a Bahrain defender and he let it bounce twice before firing in a rocket shot that exploded into the top corner from all of 25 yards.

We could not get the winner and now it would all come down to a nervy second leg in Manama just four days later. From that point when the ball sailed into the net for our vital equalising goal, I looked up and said to people around me: 'We are going to this World Cup.' However, nobody was confident and there was a bit of negativity among many of the squad. They were worried it would be tough playing Bahrain on their home ground, particularly when they only needed a 0-0 draw to qualify on away goals.

I spoke with the players and reiterated that we *would* go to the World Cup and that I had waited 16 years for that opportunity.

In Manama, there was a stifling heat inside the stadium and the local fans were hostile and fanatical. There were 35,000 inside the ground, including a healthy number of our own fans who had made the trip from Trinidad and

Tobago. Seeing our fans and hearing the noise they made was very welcome and helped us. The first half was nervy for both sides and we suffered an early setback when Chris Birchall, who had been superb in the first leg, limped off.

It remained goalless and, going into the second half, we all kept saying: 'We need to score, we need to score.' Then, just a few minutes after the restart, we got the breakthrough. Dwight Yorke sent over a great corner and my old mate Dennis Lawrence rose unchallenged to head the ball down and into the goal. There were some nervy moments, thereafter, including one when I cleared the ball off the line. Bahrain had not expected to lose and they became more frantic and frustrated as the game went on.

Leo Beenhakker (Trinidad and Tobago Manager) – *Before the match started, the players came together on the field to pray. Marvin was always the guy who took the lead in bringing them together. It was a very special moment and although I'm not such a religious guy, I said to him that there was something happening with him and the other guys, backroom staff, etc. that I felt we could not lose this match. It gave so much confidence and the feeling that we could do it.*

Along with the desperation and anxiety shown by the Bahrain players, the crowd began to show their frustration, especially near the end. As Yorke and Latapy tried to run down time down at a corner, there was a bit of aggravation and a wild tackle that almost caught Dwight. Objects started appearing on the pitch, thrown from the stands. Bahrain thought they had scored the equaliser when one of their players kicked the ball out of the hands of our keeper Kelvin Jack, but it was correctly disallowed. Then, Kelvin made a wonder save in the dying seconds, tipping a net-bound shot over the bar. We defended so well, fighting for every ball like warriors – Soca Warriors! The more the Bahrain players lost their discipline, the more we managed ours and controlled the game.

Leo Beenhakker (Trinidad and Tobago Manager) – *Marvin is a real defender – a born defender and every striker that plays against him has a very bad day! Many people appreciated him when he came back from serious injury and made himself available for the World Cup. He and his pal Dennis Lawrence were always together. They roomed together – Dr Jekyll and Mr Hyde I called them. They were always together 24 hours, always instilling fun in the group. He is a happy fun-loving guy and it says something about the way he is living, but on the field, he was as safe as the Bank of England. He always gave 120%, defending his pride and the jersey of his country. Fans appreciate that kind of commitment.*

When the final whistle went, I was ecstatic. It was the greatest day in my football life – one on which I took a major step towards fulfilling a 16-year dream to play for my country at the World Cup finals. The result was also a testament to the impact Leo Beenhakker had made with his organisation and the team spirit he had built in the camp.

The result was welcomed back home in typical Trinidad and Tobago fashion, with a lot of partying and a carnival. In fact, the next day was declared a public holiday by the head of government. The players all flew back to join the celebrations, but I could not be with them. Rangers were due to face Celtic in a crucial league match three days later and I had promised Alex McLeish I would return in time for the game. Sadly, it was not a great end to the week, as Rangers lost 3-0, but the celebrations continued back home in Trinidad and Tobago. We had become the smallest country to qualify for a World Cup, an honour we would hold until Iceland reached the finals in 2018.

The achievement of our team in qualifying was celebrated not only in Trinidad and Tobago, but across the whole of the Caribbean. No team from the region had qualified for the final stages of the World Cup since 1998, when Jamaica reached the tournament hosted by France. Prior to that, only Haiti (1974) and Cuba (1938) had made it. The atmosphere in Trinidad and Tobago leading up to the finals was buoyant and the expectation levels rose when the draw was made by FIFA in December 2005, a month after we played Bahrain. It put us into Group B alongside England, Sweden and Paraguay. It was exciting and we could not wait to get to Germany to meet them all.

Following the draw, Leo arranged a number of friendlies to prepare the team for the tournament. We played Iceland on 28 February 2006 on a cold evening at Queens Park Rangers' Loftus Road ground. We won comfortably by 2-0, with Yorke scoring both goals. Some of the guys complained about how cold it was! By then, I was acclimatised to British weather. That would be the last victory we would have ahead of the tournament, with a series of poor performances following that Iceland game.

A draw against Peru was followed by defeats by Wales (2-1), Slovenia (3-1) and the Czech Republic (3-0). These results were not ideal going into the tournament, especially with that last setback coming just a week before we were due to face Sweden in our World Cup opener. However, Beenhakker was unconcerned and told us not to worry. He explained he had deliberately organised the games against the Czechs and Slovenia to get us used to the faster and more physical approach of European sides. It gave us a taste of the quality we would face in the tournament.

After the Czech match, we flew from Prague straight to our camp in Germany and we were unprepared for the amazing reception we received when we arrived at our base in Rothenburg. The mayor came to Bremen to meet our flight and escort us to the town, where he made a formal and official welcome on a stage in the middle of the square. There to greet us was a band with steel drums and our bus carried the slogan 'Here Come The Soca Warriors'. There were around 3,000 German people there, alongside some Trinidadians who had arrived to give us support. We knew that they were turning the town into a 'little Trinidad' and our flag hung from every building.

We all signed the city's 'golden book' and we were then presented with gifts of ancient arrows and spears, in keeping with our nickname as the 'Soca Warriors'. They had done everything to make us feel welcome, with everyone carrying little Trinidad and Tobago flags.

It was a fabulous introduction to the tournament and welcome to Germany. I had played in most of the friendlies and was looking forward to getting going in the tournament. Although the results had not gone for us, I was feeling good in the games. The countdown was on and I already knew I would be playing in the opening game against the Swedes. Then, 48 hours before kick-off, my worst fears were realised when I fell awkwardly in training, damaging my knee. It was a different injury from the ACL problem I had experienced back in Scotland, but I knew it would be difficult to recover in time.

I went to the hospital with the doctor and did some work as part of the recovery process. Leo said he would give me a bit of time and would not make a decision until

24 hours before kick-off. I kept praying that it would heal. Eventually, we had to concede that I could not play, as Leo felt it was too much of a risk in such an important match. I was told that it would take around a week for my knee to recover, meaning I was likely to miss the second game against England, too. It was so disappointing. One minute I was in the team, the next I was not and was left to sit it out on the sidelines.

In the lead-up to the tournament, I had been subjected to a lot of physical checks and came through everything in good shape. I had even played on lots of different surfaces, including AstroTurf, with no problems. The training accident was just one of those things and it was unfortunate that it happened just before we travelled to Dortmund for that first game, which would be played at Signal Iduna Park.

Beenhakker was under no illusions that the task facing us in the tournament would be a difficult one. However, we wanted to perform well and not disgrace ourselves or the country.

The boys did well in the match against Sweden, earning a goalless draw. The team had to contend with Henrik Larsson and a young Zlatan Ibrahimović, but we were well organised, tackled hard and posed a threat in attack. We earned a lot of respect for that performance, as we were underdogs going into the match. Shaka Hislop had come in for Kelvin Jack in goal and had a marvellous game. He had been pulled in after Jack went down with a calf strain just ten minutes before the kick-off. For Shaka to play so well with little time to think of the task ahead was all the more remarkable. There had not even been time for him to get his eye in through a warm-up. It was simply a case of getting thrown in at the deep end. After a nervy start, he then turned it on with some fantastic saves that kept Sweden at bay and frustrated their every attack. It was not all about Shaka, though, because the whole team played well, led by captain Dwight Yorke, who played deeper than his usual club role at Manchester United and worked tirelessly, defending well when we needed him to.

Although Dwight liked to enjoy himself and party, he was a great trainer and was very fit. His attitude helped pull us through that match against Sweden. After the final whistle, Dwight and his team-mates went to our fans to take the applause. For the Swedes, there was a feeling of disappointment that they had not taken all three points, but we were more than happy with that start.

By the time the England game came around five days later, I still had not recovered enough to play. I was hopeful I would be able to return for the final match of the group stage against Paraguay, but I had to sit on the touchline and watch the game against England unfold. Again, Shaka was on top form and defied England, whose team included the likes of David Beckham, Steven Gerrard, Frank Lampard and Michael Owen. Then, with just seven minutes to go, Peter Crouch climbed above

Brent Sancho to head the ball into our net. Brent, a Rastafarian, later complained that he could not get to the cross because Crouch pulled his hair. In the dying minutes, Steven Gerrard sealed it for England with an unstoppable shot from outside the area. It had been a valiant fight, but we lost and our chance of qualifying from the group had all but gone.

We only had that solitary point from the Sweden game to show for our efforts in the first two games, but we had shown that we were not just there to make up the numbers. As it turned out, our group was the lowest scoring, despite many people believing we would be in for some heavy defeats. We had reached the finals on merit and the results in our first two games showed we had a decent team by any standards. We continued that into the Paraguay game in what would be our final match of the tournament.

I continued working hard in a bid to get fit and I was available for the match, but the manager did not put me on. There were three substitutions, but we were chasing the game after losing a goal after 25 minutes when Brent Sancho scored an own goal. We eventually went down 2-0. I had to be content with being on the bench again, but I felt that I was part of it all and no one can take that away from you. Had I not been injured, I would have played, but these things happen and it had a purpose. Despite not featuring on the pitch, I had a fantastic time.

Looking back, the team acquitted itself well and we did not disgrace ourselves against three nations who had a proven track record at that level. Ultimately, we lacked firepower and failed to register a single goal, but the World Cup was a great experience. Beenhakker had been excellent for us and instilled discipline and belief in the squad. With a little more luck, the results might have gone our way, but what a fantastic journey it had been to the finals, playing something like 20 games on the way.

Beenhakker went on to become Trinidad and Tobago's technical director, looking to build upon the success of taking the team to the World Cup finals. I think everyone hoped that our performances and the enthusiasm of the nation over our qualification would inspire the next generation to progress, but, sadly, that did not happen.

After the tournament ended, there was the sad aftermath when the players believed that promises on bonuses had not been fulfilled. It soured it for many of the players and the situation rumbled on for years. The background was that the players agreed with the national federation the fee they would receive for their World Cup efforts. The sum due to them was based on a number of factors, including the number of appearances each player made. Ultimately, the government themselves paid an out-of-court settlement to us, without prejudicing our recovery of the money due from the Trinidad and Tobago Football Association.

The man at the centre of it all was Jack Warner, who had been the federation's financial adviser. There was still a lot of money apparently unaccounted for. Some of the players pursued it through the courts, winning their cases, but still the money did not appear. It is something I have not worried too much about, because that is the way things work in Trinidad. I did not expect to see any of the money, so I have not got too wrapped up in all the legalities.

Setting aside these financial issues, it was a wonderful experience to help my country get to the finals for the first time and, although I did not play, it was fantastic to be part of it all. The qualification process had started off badly, with one point for the first three games. But after Beenhakker came in, we turned things around and our final matches leading us through the qualification phase were incredible. Ever since watching the ill-fated qualification match back in 1989, it had been my dream to help Trinidad and Tobago make it and I had prayed it would happen. It was a dream fulfilled and one of the greatest experiences of my life.

Chapter Eight

A Football Odyssey

WHEN I returned from the World Cup in Germany, I was a free agent and looking for another club. I still had to recover from the injury I sustained on the eve of the tournament, so there would be no immediate return. After leaving Rangers, I knew that I would not hit the same heights again, but I wanted to continue playing for as long as I could. I was just 30 and had many years ahead of me. Indeed, it had been a dream to play until I was 40, if possible.

Aside from football, there were other things happening in my life. In the middle of September 2006, I was ordained as a minister at the Zion Praise Centre in Kirkcaldy. This would allow me to take services and also to conduct weddings and communions for the congregation. Since then, I have conducted several marriages, some personal funerals and a few christenings. I had been training for the ordination under Pastor Joe and stepped in for him when he was away, so it was a natural progression for me. When the news was announced to the press, the pastor commented: 'Marvin has been a beacon of light for this church for the last seven years and he is so passionate about his work. We are happy to accept anyone who comes along to the congregation; even if it is through football, they will get to hear our message. Marvin works tirelessly for his church and we are proud to have him here. I was away in America recently and Marvin did a very good job while I was away, so I decided he was now ready.'

It was a wonderful honour for me, but I also had to find a club to continue my football career. Former Dundee United and Scotland star Maurice Malpas had just become manager at Motherwell and he made an enquiry about me. I did not really feel that it would work out, because I knew that I would fail a medical. However, things had already started moving elsewhere, with a possible return to Raith Rovers emerging. Gordon Brown, who was the UK chancellor of the exchequer at the time and would go on to become prime minister, was a well-known fan of the club. He contacted me through the church secretary. The club had slipped into the Second Division and Brown wanted to do what he could to get them promoted.

Brown was a Fife man and had a long association with Kirkcaldy. He had attended Kirkcaldy High School and his father was minister of the Church of Scotland in the town. When Brown was not working in Westminster, he was at his home in North Queensferry and he always came along to the games at Stark's Park whenever he could.

When the club's fortunes had plummeted further in 2005, he stepped in with some other influential locals. He was seeking a community buyout and invested some money himself into the project. The takeover of the club was launched off the back of a campaign named 'Reclaim the Rovers', which ensured community shareholdership and representation on the board. He bought shares with many other fans, raising £200,000 to help the supporters' trust that formed part of the bid. The change in ownership was not reflected in a change in fortunes for the team, however. They finished seventh in the Second Division and no nearer to the promotion they desperately wanted.

Brown's plans for the club for the following season included bringing me back to Stark's Park and, after he had spoken with Paster Joe and the secretary, we arranged to meet at the church. He brought along Craig Levein to the meeting, which was held at the end of September 2006. The club had just appointed the former Cowdenbeath, Hearts and Leicester City boss as manager, replacing Gordon Dalziel, who had not enjoyed a good start to the 2006/07 campaign. It was clear from the meeting that they seriously wanted me to come to the club. Brown outlined his hopes for the future. He told me that he wanted to build Raith Rovers up again and that I would be a good figurehead for the team.

Craig Levein later said that he did not expect me to sign, but I had made no secret of the fact that I loved my time at Stark's Park and, of course, Kirkcaldy was a happy place for me. I still lived in the town, so it had all come together ideally.

The overall deal we discussed was a good and interesting one. I would get a three-year contract and, as part of the deal, the club would establish the Marvin Andrews Youth Development Trust in Kirkcaldy. That was what appealed to me most. The trust got off to a good start and, as it was part of Brown's plans for the revitalisation of the area, it did rely on the impetus he would bring to it. When he started to pursue leadership of the Labour Party and the post of prime minister, we did not see him so often. Sadly, the initiative lost its momentum and faded.

It certainly helped that Brown led the orchestrations, because I could see that this was a serious proposition. I am not political at all, but I knew from my meetings with him that he was honourable and that I could trust him. He said that my returning was a symbol of the club's rebirth and the initiative with the youth development trust would highlight that Raith Rovers was truly a community club.

Levein succinctly discussed the situation the club was in. He said it had been battered around a bit and needed enthusiasm to drive the doom and gloom away. I felt I owed the club a lot for giving me a start in professional football and, as far as the trust was concerned, it would give me a chance to help kids make something of their lives. So many in the town had become caught up in drink and drugs. They had gone astray, but I was keen to get them off the streets. It would not all be about football, as I realised that some might want to express themselves in other ways. I also wanted to help them realise the role God could play in their lives.

We would kick off the whole initiative with football nights held at Kirkcaldy High School Community Facility. The first of these was held for kids aged between 13 and 18, on 2 March 2007. Both Raith Rovers and Cowdenbeath were represented, with players and coaching staff attending. There were many others backing the plan and I was delighted by the response we got from the kids. I really felt I was putting something back into the community. I still attend schools and community groups, but not under the original trust.

The establishment of the youth trust had obviously been important to me but, despite this and the persuasive words of Gordon Brown, I did not make the decision to return to Raith Rovers solely on the basis of what he told me. As I had always done, I took the decision to God and I knew that he wanted me back at the club. While Motherwell and many other clubs had shown interest in me, I never believed that joining them was part of God's plan. When I signed for Raith Rovers on 4 October 2006, it completed a journey that had come full circle. This is where my career in professional football had begun nine years earlier. I knew that I was once again where God wanted me to be.

As soon as I joined, the culture shock immediately set in. Our first training session was in torrential rain in the public park, a far cry from the luxury of Rangers' Murray Park. On the field, I could see that the standards of the play had dropped from my previous stint with the club and the overall quality of football was poor in the Second Division. Having come from Rangers, where I had good players around me and more time on the ball, this was all run-run-run, hustle-hustle-bustle.

Craig Levein, who did not have a contract at Raith Rovers, only lasted two months before he left to become manager at Dundee United. His agreement with the club was that if a bigger opportunity came in, he would be free to move on. He had only enjoyed one victory, which came in his first game as boss. Despite his short tenure, I enjoyed working with him. Everyone at Raith Rovers respected him and realised that, because of his stature in the game, his time at the club would likely be limited. He was excellent tactically and I built up a good relationship with him because he respected what I had achieved at Rangers. As a former Raith Rovers fan, he was so happy to be at Stark's Park, but when the opportunity came along to move to Tannadice, the pull was too strong for him to resist.

The new manager would be John McGlynn, who, ironically, had been coach at Hearts under Craig Levein. I found him to be an awesome man. He was a deep-thinking, straight-talking man who had been around the block a few times. He knew the game well and had the ambition that a club like Raith Rovers needed. The club wanted to get back into the SPL and so did he. It was not plain sailing for me at the start, as it seemed that I did not fit into the system that he planned for the team. He also had to adjust to my bubbly personality and how he could reconcile that with the serious role he had at hand. As I sat on the bench, there was some chatter as to why the club had brought me to the club in the first place. When the performances dipped, he changed his formation to build the defence around me. Whether through my influence or not, the changes signalled an improvement and I was back in my place. Things were good again in my happy place.

The team rallied under McGlynn's stewardship and the team fought to third in the championship, narrowly missing out on promotion. We had a good spell near the end of the season, going on a seven-game unbeaten run and had six clean sheets. We finished strongly, with just two defeats in the last 16 matches, but we were too far behind to catch the leaders. We ended up third and in a play-off spot, but we lost out 3-1 on aggregate to Stirling Albion, who had finished above us in the table.

The next season was more of the same as we fought for the automatic promotion spot but again had to be content with third place and a play-off position. This time it was Airdrie who defeated us, winning the semi-final 4-2 on aggregate. I had missed much of the second half of the season through injury. I had sustained further damage to my knee in a game against Ayr United at Somerset Park on 15 December 2007. Ironically, I had scored in that game, but afterwards my knee swelled up like a balloon. After missing a few games, I came back into the team, but the injury persisted. I knew that at some stage I would need an operation. This time, I did not need to rely on my faith. I had achieved everything I had wanted to do in football and I had nothing more to prove.

I left Raith Rovers in May 2008, as there was nothing more I could do for them at that time and my contract had ended. I arranged for my operation with a top orthopaedic surgeon in Bradford. The same consultant had success with former Manchester United and England star Wes Brown. Since I was not attached to any club, I paid for the operation myself. It was a huge success and I then started the long road of rehabilitation. Raith Rovers were really good to me and offered their facilities for me to train.

During that rehabilitation period, which lasted almost nine months, Raith boss John McGlynn had been watching me and reckoned I had reached a stage where I could still do a job for the club. He signed me up as a trialist and I played in a 1-0 win over East Fife in March 2009. I lasted the full 90 minutes, showing that I had recovered from the operation. I was offered another contract by the club on 11 March 2009. I was delighted to sign it, with the term taking me up to the end of the 2008/09 season. It was to be my third and final stint with Raith Rovers, the club that had first given me the chance to play professionally in Scotland. I played the last ten matches of that season, which would turn out to be a momentous one for the club. We won the title with a 1-0 win against Queen's Park at Hampden on 2 May 2009, clinching promotion to the Scottish First Division. A goal in the first minute was enough to see us home and dry.

It was fabulous for the club after it had endured such hardships since relegation. At last, after going close in the previous seasons, the title win repaid the fans and investors for their faith and support. It was nice to finish on such a high with Raith Rovers. The next week, we were presented the trophy after a dull 0-0 draw against Arbroath. As we celebrated on the field in front of our home fans, I unveiled another T-shirt, with the words 'Jesus Christ Has Done It For Me Again'. It was such a fine way to end my time with the club – one that had given me many happy memories.

I could have remained with Raith for the next season, but I got a call in the close season from Billy Reid, the manager at Hamilton Academical. They were an SPL side who had held their own in the top league after being promoted at the start of the previous season. However, they were going into the new season with problems at centre-back due to injuries, suspensions and transfers. They offered me a short-term contract in July 2009 and I signed for them. I was almost 34 and the opportunity may have been my last to play in the Scottish Premier League. I did not want to turn it down, even though I knew I was coming in simply as backup.

Although Billy Reid made it clear to me at the beginning that I was a stopgap signing, I did expect to get more game time than I did. I found it tough when I did get my chance, because I was still recovering from the operation on my ACL, but it was a chance to say my farewell to the SPL and I enjoyed my experience with the club.

Probably the highlight of my time there was when Hamilton faced Rangers at Ibrox. I was only listed on the bench, but when I came out for the warm-up, it was an emotional moment when the Rangers fans got to their feet and sang my name for five minutes. I only played a couple of matches before drifting out of the picture. Queen of the South approached me to play on a short-term loan basis and Hamilton agreed to release me. I met the Dumfries side's manager, Gordon Chisholm. He told me he needed me to fill in for a month while two of his key defenders, David Lilley and Stephen McKenna, were suspended. He said they needed my experience and my strength in the air. I would not need to travel down to Dumfries for training, as the club allowed me to train in Glasgow. I travelled to and from training with Joe Hamill, who stayed in Edinburgh.

I made my debut for them in a 2-1 win against Greenock Morton a few days after signing in December

2009. I hadn't played a match in three months before the Morton game. I had been involved in bounce games, but that's very different from the tempo and pressure of a real match. I played well and received some nice reviews, but bad weather then curtailed football for the next two weeks. It left me kicking my heels for a fortnight until I returned in a 2-2 draw with Partick Thistle at Firhill. Before the end of the January transfer window, Gordon Chisholm had indicated he wanted me to sign another deal. It all depended on Hamilton and, thankfully, they released me. He offered me a six-month contract to the end of the 2009/10 season. Chisholm commented: 'I'm glad I've got him signed up again and I think he'll be a valuable acquisition. He only managed two games during that loan spell but he impressed me in that relatively short space of time.'

I spent most of the time on the sidelines when Lilley and McKenna came back from suspension. I was just waiting for the call whenever they needed me.

At the end of March, Chisholm left to take over at Dundee, taking his coach, Billy Dodds, with him. Afterwards, Kenny Brannigan took over as boss. Minor injuries and bad luck restricted my appearances, but the team did relatively well and finished in fourth place in the Scottish First Division. When my contract with Queen of the South finished at the end of the season, I started taking some training sessions at Stark's Park to help out Raith Rovers. Then another opportunity came right out of the blue in the close season.

It was August 2010 when I was approached about a possible move to Wales to play for Wrexham. My old Trinidad and Tobago team-mate Dennis Lawrence had played for them from 2001 to 2006. His agent was a guy called Mike Berry, who had negotiated deals for many of the players from our homeland. I spoke to each of them. I had grown up with countryman Hector Sam, who had left the club in 2005 after five good years. Then there were both Carlos Edwards and Silvio Spann, whom I knew and who also played with the club. They all told me that it was a good club and that I should sign. Even when I walked into the club's Racecourse Ground, I saw the Trinidad and Tobago flag flying above the Kop and it made me feel welcome.

The manager was former Wales and Liverpool star Dean Saunders. They were looking to beef up the centre of their defence and I was offered and signed a short-term contract. They were a Conference Premier club at the time and looking to get promotion. I felt that I had plenty of football left in me and I knew this would be a good place to play. When I signed, the manager told the press: 'He has had a bit of an unsettled time in Scotland in the past couple of years but he just wants to play football and I'm sure he can do a great job for us. He's not 100 per cent fit just yet and needs a couple of weeks to get up to speed. I've told him about our plans and our ambitions during the time he has trained with us and he likes it here. He wants to be part of our plans to try and win promotion this season and I'm convinced he is the right man at the right time for us.'

Dean Saunders was great, giving me time off when he could, because he knew how important my faith was to me. He allowed me to travel back at the weekends after games and not report for training until the Tuesday. I would take the club car as far as Wigan, then get the train from there all the way back to Kirkcaldy. It allowed me time to make the church meetings on a Sunday. If I left Kirkcaldy around 6pm, I could be in Wrexham fresh and ready for training on the Tuesday morning.

I had a fabulous time at Wrexham and we had a good team. Indeed, it gave me a new lease of life on the field and I was playing with the enthusiasm I had when I first arrived in the UK. There was already a bit of experience in the side in the shape of Frank Sinclair, an English-born Jamaican who had made a name for himself, most notably with Chelsea. He would be my centre-back partner. Almost immediately, we formed a great partnership.

I settled into the side well and Saunders extended my contract from its original six months, through to the end of the season. He said: 'Marvin has earned his extended deal after playing in all but five games so far this season and has one goal to his credit. I think he has done well for us. Obviously he can't play like Rio Ferdinand, but he is very experienced. He wins plenty of headers in defence and he is a great character to have around the place. You can see just why he was so highly regarded by the fans at his previous clubs. Just his presence is intimidating to the opposition and he shows no fear in his play. He is a big part of this team and I'm delighted that he will be with us for the remainder of the season.'

Despite a poor start to the season, we pushed the club all the way into the play-offs. I suffered a hamstring injury near the end of the season and missed out on these vital matches in which we went down 5-1 on aggregate against Luton Town. Despite missing out on the drama at the end of the season, my experience at Wrexham was great.

I was offered the chance to stay on for another season, which suited me. I was comfortable in Wrexham and was also preaching the Gospel at a church there, which was another reason I loved being there. I actually got involved with the church that my fellow countryman Silvio Spann attended when he was there and they allowed me to share my knowledge and spread the word of God.

In the following season, Saunders moved on to Doncaster Rovers and I decided to leave, too. I was in the latter stages of my career, so it did not make sense to remain there much longer when I might not play regularly. Things then went quiet on the football front until, out of the blue, I got a call from Jimmy Lindsay, whom I knew from my time at Raith Rovers. Jimmy used to help out in the backroom at the club and did a bit of coaching at youth level. He was manager of Junior side Kirkintilloch Rob Roy and he wanted me to join them for a month or so until something better materialised. He knew that I was between clubs and was keeping myself fit, so it was an opportunity. The term 'Junior' refers to the level of football played below the senior league clubs, not the age of the players. The closest equivalent would be non-league football in England.

When he put the proposal to me, my reaction was 'Why not?' and I thought I would give it a try. I did not know where Rob Roy played until Lindsay pointed out that they were from Kirkintilloch and I had driven through it every time I had travelled to Murray Park while with Rangers.

There was a bit of a culture shock playing at that level, but there were some good teams, with players who had come from the professional game. I also had to deal with many players who were keen to prove themselves against me.

It was an okay experience, playing against the likes of Auchinleck Talbot in the Scottish Junior Cup, although I found it strange playing at these Junior grounds. They were exactly the kind of ground I had played on when I started my career and here I was, back again in the same type of venues. The surfaces were mostly all right, but Rob Roy's Adamslie Park was like a cowfield – one of the worst I had ever played on. I gather that it had once been a great surface but, when I played there, it was a quagmire. I could feel my feet sink deep below the surface and I worried that I might end up with a broken ankle. I gave it three months, then decided I had had enough.

Afterwards, Jimmy Lindsay commented that I had given the club a boost and had taught the players a lot, so it was nice to have made an impact in a short spell with them.

I returned to training with Raith Rovers, again waiting to see where God would next direct me on my football odyssey. I did not imagine that one of my next matches would be back at Ibrox, but that is exactly what happened. I was invited to play in a legends game on 30 March 2012, when Rangers would play the former stars of AC Milan.

The club was going through real problems after going into administration a month earlier. We felt it was important to show that the former players were all behind the club in the hope that we would help it get back on its feet. As I watched the problems unfold for Rangers, I prayed that it would work out fine. A great person is not known by where they are, but by what they have come through to get to where they are. That is how greatness is measured and in Rangers' case, if you look at what the club came through compared to where they are today, it is magnificent. For me, that is what greatness is. Yes, you can win a lot of trophies, but greatness is judged when you are going through a difficult time and it is how you respond to that. That is what makes Rangers absolutely amazing. You just have to applaud it. It shows the greatness of the fans and the club as a whole. As long as they have fans like these, Rangers will never die.

The match against AC Milan was the first opportunity for us, as players, to put a little back into a club that had been so important to our lives. When I was growing up in Trinidad and Tobago, I would always watch Italian football on TV and I really admired the AC Milan and Inter teams of that time. Seeing guys like Franco Baresi, Paolo Maldini and Alessandro Costacurta playing was an education and it was wonderful to get the chance to play with them on a field that held so many happy memories for me. Of course, I also got the chance to play alongside and share a dressing room with some Rangers legends like Brian Laudrup, Paul Gascoigne, Ally McCoist and Mark Hateley.

After playing alongside such elevated stars of the game, my next experience in football was slightly less glamorous. I had kept myself fit by attending the gym regularly and also putting in some stints training at Raith Rovers when I got a call from Todd Lumsden, who was manager at Albion Rovers. They were struggling in the Scottish Second Division and he was looking for me to come in for a short spell. He asked if I could help them avoid relegation. He also wanted me to get the attitude of the players right and try to help the younger boys in the team.

That was at the start of 2013 and I went on to play just 13 matches with them. I could not do anything to prevent the inevitable and they finished well adrift. However, if they had taken the chances they created in games, they could easily have saved themselves. Todd said that I had been a 'standout' and wanted me to commit for another season, but I felt I had done all I could with them. I was 37 now and I knew that I did not have much more football left in me, even if I fulfilled my objective of playing until I was 40.

Another of the legends games that came up in May 2013 featured Manchester United as opponents. They brought up the likes of Peter Beardsley, Dion Dublin, Henning Berg and my old friend Dwight Yorke. We beat them 4-1, earning some cash for the Rangers Charity Foundation and UNICEF. There were other attractive offers coming in to play in what might be considered 'fun' games, often for charitable purposes.

One that did not fall into that category, but was slightly different from the norm, was the chance to play in a legends tournament in the Hong Kong Sevens in May 2013. In our final group match, we lined up against Ajax, who had top stars like Jari Litmanen, Aron Winter and Kenneth Perez in their line-up. We had the likes of Michael Mols, Charlie Miller, Andy Goram, Arthur Numan, Jorg Albertz and Derek Ferguson in ours, so we had a pretty good side. We eventually lost 3-2, but I managed to score two goals in the final, the second coming after I ran half the length of the field.

I had not given up on playing competitive football, however, and a chance to get back into it again came in the close season in 2013. Dick Campbell, the inimitable

Forfar Athletic boss, came in to sign me and what a great experience that was. Having played with a few teams that struggled at the wrong end of the table, Forfar were decent and challengers for promotion. I was playing regularly for them and putting in some good performances. Campbell was a good manager, too, so there was a feelgood factor around the club.

I loved the whole experience, although it was bittersweet when we played against Rangers in a Viaplay Cup group-stage match. The game was played on Saturday, 3 August 2013 and it seemed that the whole town was in the ground, as well as a good proportion of Rangers fans who managed to scramble a ticket. The ground at Station Park was at its restricted capacity of just over 4,000. Having gone through administration and been demoted to the Scottish Third Division, the Rangers team was a shadow of the one I knew. They were still crippled by a year-long transfer embargo that lasted until September, so none of the new signings they had made in their rebuilding were available for the match. However, there were still some great players in their side, including Lee Wallace and Lee McCulloch.

It was a big match for Forfar, as they were looking to exorcise the ghosts of previous cup defeats against Rangers in the semi-final of the League Cup in 1978 and the Scottish Cup in 1982. It was a spirited performance from Forfar and we were in control of the game virtually throughout after taking the lead through Gavin Swankie after only nine minutes when he lobbed Rangers keeper Scott Gallacher.

Fraser Aird managed to get an equaliser for Rangers six minutes from time, when he stooped low to head in the rebound after Andy Little had struck the bar with a header. When the game went into extra time, many expected the Ibrox side to go on and win, but our goalscoring hero Swankie stepped up to get the winner just five minutes from the end.

Afterwards, Dick Campbell, who they called 'The Bunnet' because that was his usual headgear, said: 'I don't think we've had a better result in our history. It's as good as anything I've done as a manager. You saw how much our players wanted it and we never stopped passing the ball. Each and every one of them was magnificent. We have always had teams here full of character and the players have just made their manager a very proud man.'

Even though the result was gained by defeating my old club, it was a special one that I savoured. There was a lot of focus on me during my time there, as I still carried that reputation of having played for Rangers, but I enjoyed the experience. Even now, whenever I go to Forfar, I am regarded as something of a legend with them, which is nice. Dick Campbell was a good manager, who I loved playing under. He had a great spirit in a side that had been put together from modest resources but was a good team.

After a year with Forfar, by which time I was 38, I moved on once again at the instigation of Barry Wilson, who I had played with at Livingston. He had been an unbelievable player for us and when he hung up his boots, he was appointed manager at Elgin City, who were in the Second Division. I joined them on 10 August 2014 on the understanding that I would not have to live in the city, instead travelling up by car to Perth, where I was collected by others heading north on matchdays. I had played my first three games with them as a trialist, scoring a goal against Annan Athletic and also winning two man-of-the-match awards. On the back of that, they offered me a year-long deal, which I was delighted to accept.

One of the matches that comes readily to mind from my time there was when we met Bo'ness United in the third round of the Scottish Cup. We had drawn the first match 4-4 at our Borough Briggs ground after being pegged back from a 3-0 first-half lead. In the replay at Bo'ness, we lost 5-4, although I did score a goal to bring us back into things when we were 4-1 down. We rallied, but just failed to get the equaliser. Even though we lost that match, I was becoming something of a hero up in the town and it was a great experience for me. Their supporters were wonderful, but I knew I was nearing the end of my career.

Barry Wilson left the club in November 2014 after losing that match to Bo'ness. It had all become too much for him and he was replaced by Jim Weir. That essentially ended my hopes of continuing, as the new boss was keen to change things. I had played 17 games with Elgin, but had reached the stage where I had to move on. I was still keen to play until I was 40, providing that clubs were prepared to take me on. However, I was not looking for teams to take me on unless they believed I could do a job for them. I believed that every club I played for would agree that I did help them out and I thought I might have one last move in me.

When I left Elgin City, I was 39 and I reflected on where football had taken me. That club figures highly in my great footballing memories, if not for the quality of the game, but for the place itself. I will always fondly remember my time there in that lovely little town. This footballing odyssey was opening my eyes to what Scotland had to offer beyond its central belt and away from football.

I left Elgin in January 2015, before my contract had ended, when I got the chance to join Montrose. They would be the 14th club I would play for. They were in dire straits, sitting above Elgin, who were bottom of the table, but my former club had games in hand that could force Montrose to the bottom. Relegation would have taken them into non-league football, which would have been disastrous for the club. Their manager, George Shields, was desperate to get me in to shore up his defence and provide some added experience. He offered me a contract to the end of the season. I played a trial match against Arbroath just after New Year and we drew 2-2. Afterwards, George came out in the press to applaud my performance, saying: 'Marvin was magnificent against Arbroath and I am delighted to have his experience on board.'

The following week, I scored my first goal for the club in a 3-3 draw with Berwick Rangers. That had George coming out to proclaim that I was his best ever signing. Although my contract would take me through to the end of the season, things were in flux at Montrose. No sooner had I come in, George was sacked and replaced with the former Dundee United star Paul Hegarty.

The team could not pull away from the bottom of the table and relegation faced them, with a play-off against Highland Football League champions Brora Rangers their only hope of avoiding the drop. Brora got the perfect start in the two-leg affair, winning the first game 1-0 at their home ground, Dudgeon Park. Unfortunately, I scored the only goal when a shot deflected from me and ended up in the net. The return leg was played a week later at our home ground, Links Park. The stakes were enormous, with the very future of the club at stake. If they failed to overcome the 1-0 deficit, they would be relegated to the Highland League.

The enthusiasm in the town for the team was heartening. I looked around and in the crowd I could see locals representing every age group, from old men and ladies to young kids. It seemed that everyone from the town was there to see us, hoping that we could rescue the tie and retain our place in the Scottish Football League.

We managed to get the first goal eight minutes before the interval when Scott Johnson scored to level the tie on aggregate. Brora's Colin Maclean made it 1-1 just after the break, but two minutes later they were reduced to ten men when their top goalscorer, Steven Mackay, was sent off for a second yellow card. Even so, it looked for a long spell that we might not get the equaliser. Then, with 15 minutes to go, I rose to meet a corner and powered the ball into the net. It was now 2-2 in aggregate and, just 90 seconds later, Garry Wood scored from 35 yards to secure the priceless winning goal. The match characterised why people play football. The game turned on its head in two minutes.

I was delighted to make some amends for my own goal in the first leg and the fans treated me as a hero for getting the equaliser in the second leg. At the end of the match, some lifted me shoulder high. The Montrose fans still hail me, saying that it was my goal that kept them up. What a wonderful day it was in front of just over 2,000 fans. I would say that it was up there with some of my best experiences in football, alongside those playing with Rangers. The relief from the fans in retaining their league status was palpable. For me, it was one of these destiny moments. God had said: 'Marvin, go save Montrose' and it certainly felt that way. I had performed at such a level that I was included in the Scottish League Two team of the year. It was a great honour and I still have the little plaque commemorating that success.

At the end of the season, with Montrose's future secured, I left the club and travelled back to Trinidad and Tobago for another charity match. This time, I would play for Liverpool! It was the Tobago Legends Challenge football tournament sponsored by British Airways and was played at the Dwight Yorke Stadium, Tobago. In the final, we met the popular Caribbean All-Stars, containing Russell Latapy, Stern John, Cornell Glen and my mate Dennis Lawrence. I actually scored five goals in the tournament, which was a nice distraction from life in the lower leagues in Scotland.

After I returned from the Caribbean, I got a call from Barry Ferguson, who had taken over as manager at Clyde. Even though I was now 39, he felt I could do a job to help him and his assistant, Bob Malcolm. They were playing in Scottish League Two, formerly known as the Scottish Second Division and renamed after league restructuring in 2014. The boys wanted my experience to help the younger team members. I trained with them and then Barry decided to offer me a contract, which I signed in September 2015. After I put pen to paper, Barry said: 'I know Marvin well and I also played with him. He's been training with us for a few weeks now and his fitness levels are good. He will provide more backup and more experience in the centre-half position. I like to have at least four players in that position in my squad. He isn't going to cost the club anything and he's a fantastic person to have in the dressing room. I don't think anyone that's played with him would disagree with that.'

I had a good start with Clyde, scoring on my debut against one of my former clubs, Elgin City. I put in some great performances. I had not lost any of my physicality and a funny conversation took place before we played Arbroath, who were the top dogs at the time. They had a young player, Simon Murray, who was hot property. I heard recently from a chap who was his agent at that time that he was panicking in case I broke the youngster's leg!

Barry had done well with Clyde and he took them into a play-off for promotion. They lost out by the odd goal over two legs against Queen's Park. At the end of the season, I had played just 13 games and I was released by the club. By now, I was 40 and I had achieved my dream of playing until that age. There were further offers for me to play on, but my body was beginning to tell me that I could not do it any more. I had not been playing many games latterly and on one bitterly cold night when I played against East Fife, I thought to myself, 'What are you doing?' I thought that my time had come and gone and that I should step aside to let some youngsters come through and enjoy the career I had had.

Instead of making a big announcement about hanging up my boots, I just drifted into the background. Although clubs continued to make enquiries, my decision had been made. I had enjoyed a wonderful career that took me to just about every part of the world. In these latter years, my odyssey had taken me to some of the footballing backwaters in Scotland. I had enjoyed it all and I finished with absolutely no regrets. The journey had taken me around Scotland, learning more about the beauty of my adopted homeland. I enjoyed all that travelling, but there would be no more in my professional career. I had used my God-given ability to its full potential and, looking back now, I have to say it was the best decision to end when I did. I have never missed the game since then and my overriding thought is: been there and done it!

I started off my career in Trinidad, playing in some pretty spartan grounds and, having played at some of the biggest venues in football, my journey had come full circle. It had ended just as it started, but what happened in between was wonderful and memorable. I had a brilliant time serving those 14 senior clubs and one junior side. Not many players can boast of such diversity in their careers, but I would not change a thing.

In November 2016, after I had hung up my boots, I received an important accolade from Raith Rovers when I was elected into their Hall of Fame. I had played 145 times for the club over three spells and scored 14 goals. One of the highlights had been when I came back for the third time and helped the club to win the Second Division title. They provided me with some great memories and I thank God every day for bringing me to Kirkcaldy and to Raith Rovers. I'm truly blessed to have played for them.

The boots may have been hung up professionally, but my enthusiasm remains undiminished when the opportunities come to pull on a jersey again for charity. On occasions, it has taken me back to Ibrox and it is always a great feeling to run out on to that pitch again and play in front of those great fans, who love the club. I still have that competitive spirit about me and I still train and look after myself, as well as doing a lot of running and keeping myself fit.

In playing with some of the legends, I have learned a bit more about the history of Rangers, too. In charity matches, I sometimes need to pinch myself when I play with some of the great names that have represented the club. I often look around the dressing room and wonder if it is really happening. I often feel humbled to be part of it all.

It has been a good career and one that I look back on with some satisfaction. Now, my life takes me away from the playing field, but football is never far away.

Chapter Nine

Managers and Players

I HAVE obviously played with many players and served a number of managers through my career. Several of these made a great impact on me and helped me develop, both as a footballer and as a person. I have probably worked under almost 30 managers in my career, from my earliest days in Trinidad until I kicked my last ball professionally with Clyde. Of them all, there is one that emerges as a standout, quite simply because of the influence he had on my career. His name will surprise many, because he was not involved in any of the triumphs I enjoyed as a player. He is Bertille St Clair, who coached the Trinidad and Tobago side in two spells – from 1997 to 2000 and 2004 to 2005. He was also the first to take the country to the Youth World Cup and it was while he was national youth coach that I first got to know him.

I can see many parallels with the way Bertille approached things with what I know of the legendary Rangers boss Bill Struth. He liked the players to be smartly dressed and to wear ties. He also preferred short hair and liked the players to look after themselves. He was very much the kind of man who focused on standards, rather than the tactical aspects of the game. He created that platform for us to be a good side, but, unfortunately, he could not take things to the next level.

Despite his old-school ways and efforts at keeping us under control, he faced problems in dealing with the traditional character of players from the islands. There were some who would try to bend the rules he laid down. Issues of timekeeping and an inclination for some players to do their own thing hindered the harmony of the team. However, despite the difficulties he faced, he had a great influence on me, working on my touch and always offering words of encouragement. It was Bertille who first told me that I could be a professional player with a good career ahead of me, if I believed in myself. He would often say: 'One day, you will get your opportunities.'

He liked both myself and Dennis Lawrence, because we were dedicated to the game and were not disrespectful to him. He was a great influence on young players and had also made Dwight Yorke the player he would turn out to be. He was 100 per cent the biggest influence on the careers of both Dennis and me. We often talk about those days playing under him. He was a great man.

Although not out of the same old-school box, my former Rangers boss Alex McLeish was another that impressed me with how he went about the job. His secret was that he was a former player himself, so he knew how players thought. He was not so much of a tactical coach – Dutchman Jan Wouters, who was an assistant coach, provided much of the technical stuff – but Alex was the great motivator. He was not the kind to get involved in shouting matches in the dressing room, but he was always there to explain to players what he expected of them on the field. His approach was based on the fundamentals of football, playing with heart and running your socks off.

In many ways, I believe that he was not appreciated by the fans, although he had the utmost respect of the players. Towards the end of his final season, which was also mine, I think he became something of an easy target when the results started to go against us. Perhaps it is only now that people are beginning to appreciate what he did for the club. To win seven major trophies and a treble at a time when the club was in the midst of austerity, cutting costs left right and centre, was amazing. He did remarkably well in his recruitment, while also losing his best players. An amazing manager and one who was so important to me.

Another of the same stature was Leo Beenhakker, my old boss with the Trinidad and Tobago national side. As I mentioned previously, what really impressed me about him was how, faced with the traditional laid-back attitude of my countrymen, he turned us into a thoroughly professional unit. Indeed, I believe that if, in previous tournaments, we had adopted that same level of professionalism that took us to the World Cup in Germany in 2006, we would have qualified for many more.

When he initially came in, we had won just a single point from three games, so he took a look at the culture and decided how he could work with what he had. Bertille St Clair had effectively lost the dressing room. One of the first things he did was to ensure that we were all operating off the same page. Until then, players would be staying in different hotels, contracted with different sportswear suppliers and turning up wearing whatever took their fancy. He immediately changed that, putting us all in the same hotel and insisting we all wear the same training gear and suits while on international duty. Players had also previously turned up for training whenever they wanted. By the time the manager had instilled his ideas, we all turned up on time, appeared for events and matches in the proper gear and were completely professional in our approach.

There were those in the squad who had been a bit rebellious, but he brought them into line and we all began to train and play with much more unity. Russell Latapy – the golden boy of Trinidad football – and Dwight Yorke could both be wayward, but Beenhakker got them to buy into his plans, bringing them back into the fold. It was so important, because they were great players and we needed them. He was also not afraid to make big decisions, dropping Russell for games when he felt he needed a change. He even left him out of the team for the second leg against Bahrain in the World Cup qualifying play-off, because he felt he needed other strengths in the match. Although he brought on Russell in the second half, it was a measure of Beenhakker's strength of character that he was prepared to make the big calls, no matter that it was the most important game we had played for years. We all respected him because he did what was necessary for the team.

He was one of the first to introduce video analysis, so going into matches we knew all about the opposing teams and the players we would face. Playing under Beenhakker for the national side was refreshing. I think we all realised that we had to change and, as a foreign manager, he was best placed to instigate the necessary changes. Had he been from Trinidad and Tobago, perhaps his words would not have resonated to the same degree, but here was a man who was well respected in the world game. His introduction to our game was hugely important and the single biggest reason why we played as one and achieved our dream of playing at the World Cup finals in 2006.

If Beenhakker was thoroughly professional and a modern style of manager with his detailed tactical analysis, then Dick Campbell was typical of the old-school bosses who still existed in parts of Scotland – but I loved him. I do not mean to denigrate him by referring to him as old school, because that was the fundamental reason of his success at Forfar Athletic.

He was so funny and built up a wonderful team spirit that helped carry us over the line against better teams, such as Rangers.

His parallel was Jim Leishman at Livingston – another carved from the same block. Both would go about their team talks with fanciful stories of the times when they were in the trenches. In Dick's case, his escapades often revolved around affixing his bayonet as he left the trench – ready for hand-to-hand fighting. Of course, neither Jim nor Dick were anywhere near the trenches in warfare, but they were trying to colourise their team talks with a bit of comical drama. They wanted their players to battle and for us to leave the dressing room with the same courage and determination, as if we had just stepped up from a trench. No one should stand in our way!

Dick's teams were not all about determination and fighting spirit, however. He knew the game inside out and his motivational strength, allied to the experience he had assembled in his side, turned us into a formidable outfit. What a manager he was – one of the game's great characters. He really took to me and I had a thoroughly enjoyable time playing under him, even if he did round on me once, having a go at my faith at the same time. Three of us travelled by car to training and submitted our expenses, each for the same car journey. When he found out, he said: 'Marvin, how can you do that when you are a man of God?' It was all good fun, of course, but was so important to the spirit he engendered in the team.

As I mentioned, Jim Leishman was another of the same type of manager. He also loved me as a person and I had huge respect for him when he came to my church. He was such a bubbly character and enormously popular in the dressing room. He helped me a lot during my time at Livingston, using his experience as a defender to offer guidance on aspects of my game.

He was such an infectious character that he never needed to shout to get his message across in the dressing room. There were the stories, like Dick Campbell's, occasionally laced with the little bits of prose that eventually characterised him. Of course, in the background was David Hay, his assistant, who would eventually take over the manager role. If Jim was the ebullient type, David was quieter and more thoughtful. He was the tactical man and obviously brought a huge amount of experience as a player into our dressing room. He would explain what was expected of us and his man-management was excellent. He and Jim were an excellent management team.

Both have done a lot in the game, but one man I met as he started out his career and who should have gone on to greater things was John McGlynn. When he came into Raith Rovers after the departure of Craig Levein, we did not automatically hit it off together. He was rather serious in his demeanour in the early stages of his time at Raith Rovers, possibly because it was his first management job. Until then, he had been operating as an assistant at Hearts, but it seemed when he came to Stark's Park he wanted to impose himself – on the job as much as on the club.

Eventually, when we got to know each other better and he needed to change things in the side, I became a fixture in his team. We got on well and I believe I helped him considerably. By then, he understood me and my bubbly disposition. Until then, I think he found it hard to reconcile that with the professional environment of a football club. It is the way I always was and, no matter what was happening around me, I have always tried to maintain that upbeat attitude to life. He would eventually learn that, despite my demeanour, I was as fully committed as anyone.

He instilled his own organisation and professionalism into the club. Prior to that, it had been chaotic and not the place I encountered when I first arrived at Stark's Park in 1997. His enthusiasm began to permeate throughout the club and we started to see the benefits in our results. He worked to get us fit and Tuesday nights were fearsome, with hard running. He was an awesome man whose easy-going character began to envelop Stark's Park, turning the staff into one big family. He eventually became boss at Heart of Midlothian, but it is a surprise that he did not go on to manage at an even higher level.

I have so much respect for John McGlynn that I consider him to be up there among the best I played under. Even after I had my operation, he kept the door open for me. Through his influence, my last period at Raith Rovers was a memorable and a happy one.

Of course, I cannot speak of my time at Stark's Park without reflecting on my first boss, Jimmy Nicholl. As I've said, my career in Scotland might never have got off the ground if he had not seen something in me and taken that chance. He was such a welcoming character in these early months of my time in Scotland and I learned a huge amount from him. As a former defender himself, he could see ways in which I could improve my approach to the game.

I think one of his strengths was his ability to understand players, having played at the top level himself. He got to know everyone well and would often have one-to-ones with us, trying to understand us as individuals, apart from our footballing ability. For that reason, his man-management was excellent and he created a happy atmosphere at the club. He had such a wonderful sense of humour. Fridays were always the most enjoyable, as he did not work us hard at the end of the week going into the weekend. However, we would play all these little fun games like the crossbar challenge. Then, of course, he had Alex Smith as his assistant and he brought so much managerial experience at the top level to assist Jimmy.

When it comes to enthusiasm, there were few who could top Dean Saunders. He was a really upbeat guy, but he was also focused. Again, like many of the bosses I've had, he came into management off the back of a good playing career. He liked to refer to his own experiences in football in his team talks, saying, 'When I played there or with them, we did …' But he was very much at home on the training field, when he would take the forwards and work with them while his assistant would work with the defenders.

He certainly looked after me well and that was typical of his character with all the players. Everyone liked him, partly because he was so switched on. Tactically, he was excellent and what really characterised him was his determination to succeed. He was a born winner.

Of the other managers I had, I was fortunate that there were no bad ones. In the latter stages of my career, when I spent short durations at some clubs, I did not really get the chance to see how the managers' skills would play out. However, they all brought something to their clubs when I was there. My old captain at Raith Rovers, Todd Lumsden, never really developed his management potential, although he could have done so much more in the game.

George Shields gave me a wonderful experience of life at Montrose and should also have done more in the game as a team boss, but it was not to be. Then there was Gordon Chisholm, who did remarkably well to take Queen of the South all the way to the Scottish Cup Final. He was not the kind of boss who would scream and shout at players, getting over his message in a quite controlled way. Tactically, he was excellent and relied on his skills, rather than being motivational.

However, of all the bosses I had, the one that could have developed a good career in management was Barry Ferguson. He had it all, but the biggest problem he faced was that he found it frustrating to have players working beneath him who did not play to the standards he was accustomed to. Barry set such high standards that he expected players to be able to do some of the things that came as second nature to him. When he realised that his early managerial career was in working with players who were so far away from him in his ability, I think he found that difficult to deal with. Having also come from a huge club, he undoubtedly found it a challenge dealing with small-club mentalities. As I mentioned before, Barry was a born winner and he really needed his team to be consistently winning.

Managers in my footballing life have come in all shapes and sizes, with every type of character, but I would not criticise any of them, because they have a difficult job. I have done some coaching, especially at the academy with the youngsters, but I never considered being a manager myself. I enjoy coaching youngsters. People have said that I am good at speaking with them and that I can relate to kids perhaps better than most. I do like to offer them encouragement in the game. It has always been the way of things for me, even when I played against younger players. I had no problem in offering guidance and encouragement to young opposition players. However, I never contemplated taking that kind of coaching into management. It was never something that interested me.

I have always been interested in how people go about their job, but it is the players I can relate to. Over the years, I have come up against hundreds of great players, but there are some that I have particularly admired in the ways in which they have gone about their work on the field.

One of the best I have played with and who I admired most is my countryman Russell Latapy. I have already explained how he could be unprofessional at times and, to an extent, that is what characterised him. However, if he had been more diligent about the way he went about his business, I firmly believe he would have been up there amongst the greatest ever players. Watching him at times was like looking at an early version of Lionel Messi.

He truly was an unbelievable footballer and people would go to watch the international side simply to see him. It was like going to see the Russell show. He was very much the golden boy of the Trinidad and Tobago team for many years. When I finally got the chance to play alongside him in the national side, I watched him in awe. He was just so skilful and everything in our play came through him. He was always the most gifted player on the pitch.

It was incredible to think that he was a drinker and smoked 20 cigarettes a day but could still turn in these wonderful performances. When he came back into the fold of the national side, he was the key to our qualification. A typically laid-back type of guy, he remains a friend to this day but, despite him having a good club career that took him to Portugal and a spell with Rangers, I do not think he was fully appreciated for what he could have achieved in the game.

I cannot talk of Russell without mentioning Dwight Yorke, who was our other star player from the period. Both had come through a similar footballing journey, introduced to the higher echelons of our game in Trinidad and Tobago at a young age. Originally from the smaller island of Tobago, he was only 17 when he broke into the international team and then got a transfer to Aston Villa at that same age. It was no surprise when Villa snapped him up after they encountered him while on a tour of the Caribbean. His transfer was huge news in the islands. He had a great career in England, culminating in three years with Manchester United. Like Latapy, he was fantastically talented, although he was more professional in the way he went about his business. He scored goals for fun as a youngster and everyone spoke of his talent.

For most players from the islands, Dwight set the standards and everyone wanted to emulate him in becoming a star in the English league. Despite his profile in football and reputation as having a lust for life, I always found him to be a quiet guy who was very grounded. A great friend and team-mate, his role in getting us to the World Cup in Germany is immeasurable.

There are a couple of others from my homeland that I have to give mention to, while recognising that I may have left out others. Stern John was a fantastic player. After rising to prominence in the United States, he got a transfer to Nottingham Forest in 1999 in a career that took him to another eight English sides over an 11-year period. What a wonderful footballer he was and a great goalscorer.

I cannot miss out my great friend and partner at the heart of the Trinidad and Tobago side – Dennis Lawrence. I first came across him when we were both youngsters in schools football. He was so frail – just a wee skinny boy. As he grew older, he became so much taller and, when I next caught up with him, I hardly recognised him as the same person. He had played central midfield, but eventually graduated to the central defensive berth. When we played together, they called us the 'twin towers'. We were both strong in the air and formed a wonderful, uncompromising partnership.

Strangely, Dennis was 27 before he got his break in UK football. When most of us played in Trinidad and Tobago, football was seen more as a sport than an occupation. It only provided a way out into a good career for a precious few, so Dennis joined the army and it was only after playing with them that he came to the notice of scouts from Wrexham. He had a decent career in the English leagues and remains in Wrexham to this day. For many, he will be forever remembered for that great goal he scored in our qualifying decider with Bahrain. I can still visualise that goal as he rose to power the ball down, through the keeper's legs and into the net.

Before I leave my countrymen and talk of other players who have impressed me, I must mention again my cousin, Shawn David. He had a God-given talent that should have taken him on to much greater things in the game. He did actually get capped, but he was born probably just a little too early to have the exposure that would take many to Europe. Like Dennis, he could not see a way that the game could provide a livelihood for him, so he joined the police back in Trinidad and he is still in the force on the island. I have no doubts that he could have had a wonderful career in football, but it was not to be. He did, however, help to stimulate my interest in the game and, for that, I am eternally grateful. What an amazing player he could have been in the UK.

I have played against many players who have impressed me to a greater or lesser degree, but one of the best was Ronald de Boer. He had left Ibrox before I arrived at Rangers, but I did play against him when I was at Livingston and what a player he was. I just could not get close to him. His movement was world-class, especially the way he used to come off the ball and slip sideways. He used to pull you into areas that you didn't want to go to. It was easy to see why he had played with Barcelona. I remember playing against him in December 2002 at Ibrox and Rangers hit us like a whirlwind. We were three down after 18 minutes and, although he was not on the scoresheet, De Boer was at the heart of just about everything in that game.

Another great player I came up against was the Czech, Jan Koller. Trinidad and Tobago played them in a friendly in June 2006, just before the World Cup. We lost 3-0 and he was immense, scoring one of the goals. After starting his career with Sparta Prague, he played with Borussia Dortmund, helping them to the Bundesliga title and the UEFA Cup. Like De Boer, he had a wonderful touch and great movement. When you expected him to head the ball, he would suddenly take it on his chest and he could move. What a wonderful player and difficult opponent.

At Ibrox, I faced a difficult strike force when we played Inter Milan in 2005. They were Obafemi Martins and Adriano. I learned a lot from Adriano, in particular when he scored against me following a corner at Ibrox. It looked to all that he had stolen a yard on me, but he gave me a push just as the ball came in and no one saw it. He was very clever, but he did not do it again. After that, I roughed him up a bit at every set piece, so that he never got the chance again. However, it was interesting to see him use his experience in these situations and I learned from that.

Against Celtic, of course, I had to deal with the likes of Henrik Larsson, who offered no real threat when he was outside the area but came alive in the box. But John Hartson was the one I faced most often. He was tough, but I gave him it back and we had some good exchanges during the game. I recall once when I just got on the end of a cross to clear with a flying header and he complimented me. It was that kind of contest. The chat was always fair and we had good physical battles.

However, in terms of real quality, I turn again to some that I played with. As I have mentioned previously, Barry Ferguson was special – a player of true class. I've mentioned Dado Prso, too, who was always a battler and what a football player! Then, of course, there was Nacho, who formed the perfect partnership with big Dado – a wonderful goalscorer. Fernando Ricksen really came into his own when Alex McLeish moved him into the midfield. I think he probably recognised that Fernando always wanted to be involved in the play and, by moving him into the middle of the park from full-back, he could get that involvement. The consummate professional, he was a wonderful captain.

Of course, there have been many others I've played with in more recent times in charity matches who have been recognised as being among the greats. The likes of Michael Mols, Artur Numan and, of course, Brian Laudrup still showed glimpses of their quality, but one player who has always impressed me with his skill is Charlie Miller. Obviously when we play now, much of the fitness has gone, but he has unbelievable talent. Although he made a name for himself at Rangers, I am sure he had the ability to have done more. Again, another wonderful footballer.

Inevitably, there will be some fans out there who read this – and, perhaps, other players – who wonder why I did not mention their particular favourites. In truth, I played with and against so many wonderful players and for so many great managers that I cannot do justice to them all in a few short paragraphs. As I reflect back on my career, it is heartening to know that so many footballing stars and characters came into my life, helping the colourful tapestry of my career. It has been an honour to know and play with them all.

Chapter Ten

Bigotry and Racism

STRANGELY, DESPITE living in Scotland, where religion can play a major part in people's lives or their judgement of others, I have rarely been asked about mine. Whether I am Roman Catholic or Protestant never seems to have entered the thoughts of the people I have met and that is how it should be. For those who may still wonder if I am one or another, they will be sorely disappointed. I consider myself neither Catholic nor Protestant. I am a Christian and I believe in Jesus Christ. That is not a get-out answer, but the fact of where my beliefs lie, in the Bible. That is what guides my everyday life.

It does not matter whether I am Protestant or Catholic, black or white. People should not be judged upon their creed or religion, but it was not always that way in Scotland. Religious divisions have existed for a long time in Scotland and certainly much longer than before I arrived.

From an early age, children have been exposed to it, with friends directed to different schools depending on their religion. Even now, the education system in Scotland has schools where Roman Catholic children go exclusively, while others attend non-denominational facilities. Segregation also found its way into the workplace, where one of the first questions at interview was often what school the applicant went to.

The question of religion has reared its ugly head in football in Scotland for many years. The two main football clubs in the country – Rangers and Celtic – have an intense rivalry, much of which is rooted in religious divisions. Rangers have been known as a Protestant club and Celtic as Roman Catholic. Their colours are blue and green respectively and many supporters will never allow themselves to be seen wearing the colours of their rivals. Many proclaim that their affiliation to their favoured club was assumed in the cradle. Some have said to me that they were 'born a Rangers fan'. An equal number proclaim the same of Celtic. However, they are wrong. They were not born to be one or the other. They were born as human beings and any beliefs or affiliations they have carried since then were assumed or taught. It is the same with every other 'religion'. You are not born into that religion, you are taught to follow it, whether it be Christian, Hindu, Muslim or whatever faith you follow.

In Scotland, and especially when I joined Rangers, I was dropped into the middle of this whole Catholic-Protestant situation. The divisions were always there and I believe there was a time when Rangers did not knowingly sign Catholic players. However, Graeme Souness smashed any sectarian policy the club may have practised when, back in 1987, he signed Maurice (Mo) Johnston. Not only was Johnston a Roman Catholic, but he had played for Celtic. The transfer sent out a huge message to everyone that Rangers would sign players, regardless of religion.

So, when I joined the club, I was surprised that, given the background, not once did anyone at Rangers ask my religion. Had they done so, then I could quite easily explain my beliefs as they remain today – that is, neither Catholic nor Protestant. They lie within the preachings of the Bible, as I have said. Many of the songs that emanated from the stands at Ibrox and Parkhead celebrated the Pope or the Queen in a quasi-religious context. I understand that they were heads of the respective Roman Catholic and Protestant churches, but nowhere are either mentioned in the Bible. The songs and these figureheads can be used almost as battle hymns among the fans. But in the Bible, there is no room for the hatred that can develop among the rival fan groups, especially when sung under the banner of religion. The Bible says 'love your enemy'. Hatred is a word of destruction. It has no room in Christian life. The fundamentals of what I believe in emanate from the teachings of the Bible, leading me to follow my life in a manner that will make me a good person.

There are many other non-Christian religions in the world, of course, including Islam, Hinduism and

Buddhism, which are all at variance with my own beliefs. Despite this, I respect the followers of other religions which are not based on a belief in God. I never forced my own beliefs upon them, but I can have an adult conversation on where we disagree. It is essentially a question of respect. I have lots of friends who are Muslim and I played with some too, but I have always respected their beliefs, even though they were completely different from mine.

As a footballer, I was frequently asked for an autograph, which I was always delighted to provide. I used to always add the words 'God Bless' after my name, until some fans asked me not to write it. I presume that they saw it as a Catholic symbol, like making the sign of the cross, which you see some players do on the playing field. I used to do that, too, but after I joined Rangers, I was advised not to do it. It did not bother me, because it was simply a gesture. My blessings come from praying and speaking with God, not offering some symbolism, so it was no trouble giving it up. I see it is more readily accepted from players at Ibrox nowadays, but it is not something I see as important to my devotion to God.

The Bible provides a good basis upon which people can lead and enjoy their lives, putting their faith in the Lord. As I said, the key word is 'respect' and that should be fundamental to all religions. We would not have much of the strife in the world if that word was adopted and applied universally. Others may follow different beliefs, but they should respect others who disagree with theirs. That leads me on to racism. Firstly, I should say that I have only twice experienced or heard of any racially motivated abuse against me in a football match.

One incident came when I played for Livingston in a match against St Johnstone at Perth in 2003. One of the opposing fans called me a 'black bastard' and was showering racial abuse on my team-mate Eugene Dadi. The offender was promptly arrested. Thankfully, he had been called out by another fan, who reported him to the police. Even after having been warned by them to cease, he continued, prompting his arrest. The individual made a court appearance and was fined £450. He had tried to justify his actions in court by saying he was passionate about his team and that saying opposition players are 'rubbish' was part and parcel of the game. That may well be the case, but the line is drawn at racial abuse. There is no reason why people should be abused based on the colour of their skin.

I understand that passion exists in the game and when fans have a fervent support for their team that it will lead to some shouting from the stands. That should not descend into racial abuse. The judgement thankfully showed that there would be no tolerance in the Scottish courts to that kind of behaviour.

On another occasion at Livingston, I read that someone in our crowd had been jailed for racially abusive language which he hurled at both Eugene and me. We never heard it, but the guy got his just reward. It is not to say that these were the only instances where I suffered some abuse, but on the playing field, especially with the big clubs, you don't really hear specific voices. When you are deeply involved in the game, all you can hear is a background buzz from the crowd. It was good to see the authorities react to a growing awareness of racism around the world and take positive action to stamp it out.

Even after joining Rangers, I called out our own fans after they abused Celtic's Bobo Balde during an Old Firm match on 8 May 2004. We lost 1-0 to a last-minute goal, but it did not justify the monkey chants he received from a small section of our fans. I had been asked to provide support to an initiative established by the authorities called 'Show Racism the Red Card'. It was set up in 1996, ironically in part through the financial assistance provided by my old Trinidad and Tobago team-mate Shaka Hislop. Following the personal episodes that I endured at St Johnstone and Livingston, I was engaged in the campaign. At the time, I highlighted that: 'Racism tried to destroy everything good in the world. You can't judge someone by the colour of their skin, their origin or because they come from a different nation or religion, especially in football.'

After being invited to become one of the campaigners, I would occasionally attend meetings to express my views. One of these was held just a day after that particular Old Firm game. I was naturally quizzed on my views on the

Balde situation and I told the press that I abhorred the treatment he had received. I highlighted that, like me, Bobo had arrived in Scotland to enjoy his football and make a living. He did not do anything to justify the abuse he received that day.

I believed that the two Old Firm clubs had a responsibility to drive out racism. They had to set a standard and parents had a role, too. Children are impressionable, especially at a young age, and must wonder why they hear monkey noises and adults calling black players names. Thankfully, the diversity of football nowadays and the success of the campaign has seen that kind of behaviour diminished.

Rangers have since, in 2020, established their own campaign to show that the club has no barriers. Called 'Everyone, Anyone', the club initiative highlighted that it was fully inclusive and showed togetherness and zero tolerance to all forms of racism. It was a major step forward in the quest to eradicate all forms of racism and intolerance.

I'm often asked to speak of my experiences in Scotland, which I know is a much more tolerant country regarding racism in football compared to some others around the world. Just a couple of years ago, Rangers' Glen Kamara suffered on-field abuse from a Czech player with Sparta Prague and, rather than be contrite, his club took a position that was quite inflammatory. Every season we read of other occurrences across Europe, with players leaving the field rather than be subjected to abuse. Indeed, in January 2024, AC Milan's Mike Maignan was subjected to racial abuse from a section of the home fans in a match against Udinese, leading to the whole Milan team walking off.

Ironically, having played the game across many continents and both with and against players of different cultures, we are at one when we are on the field. We are as brothers – black, white and coloured – all producing a game of football for entertainment and, no matter that our team-mates may be of different race and creed, we act as a single entity, a team. That probably explains why the Milan players walked off with Maignan.

We were all created in different colours but all in God's image. Football has often provided a focus for racism, but there is no room for it in life, let alone sport.

Thankfully, racism is not as prominent in Scottish football as it once was. The first black player signed by Rangers was Walter Tull, who was sadly killed in the First World War and never got the chance to play for the club. We will never know how he would have been treated by the crowds in Scotland; however, he did suffer abuse from opposing fans when he played with Tottenham, causing him to leave that club to join Northampton Town.

I first heard the story of Tull after I joined Rangers and, in many ways, it was inspirational. Like me, his roots were in the Caribbean, with his father having been born in Barbados. At the outbreak of the First World

War, he had been one of the first to join a footballer battalion. These battalions were set up to attract young men from the game into the armed conflict. Tull was to be a great soldier and he was awarded a commission in May 1917, becoming the first mixed-race combat officer in the British Army. The command caused some consternation in army circles, as it was in conflict with the 1914 Manual of Military Law, which shamefully excluded non-whites from exercising command as officers.

Sadly, after completing his officer training in Gailes on the Ayrshire coast, Tull returned to the battle. He fought in the Battle of Messines in Flanders, just four months after signing at Ibrox. He was then thrust into the third Battle of Ypres, before entering the conflict in the Somme and the Menin Road Ridge. In 1918, he was transferred to Italy before returning to Northern France for the spring offensive. Sadly, Tull was killed by machine-gun fire on 25 March 1918, near the little village of Favreuil in Pas-de-Calais. Walter's body was never recovered and he has no known grave. He was destined never to wear the blue Rangers jersey, but is rightly lauded as a hero by the club. Here was a player who fought and died for his country, yet just a short time earlier he had been tormented by racial abuse on the football field. Where is the sense in that?

Rangers also signed an Egyptian player named Mohammad Latif. Latif, who was born in Cairo in

1909, had a typically Arab complexion. He was one of the top players in his country and he helped his national side qualify for the 1934 World Cup. He competed for a football gold at the Berlin Olympics of 1936. On the day that Egypt were eliminated from the tournament, Jesse Owens won the 200m gold medal in the fastest time over the distance. Owens was another sportsman who endured racial discrimination as a result of his colour. He was snubbed at the medal ceremony by Adolf Hitler.

Latif only played twice in the first team for Rangers and the newspapers of the period provide no insight into how he was treated in these games. He became a top sports commentator back in Egypt after he hung up his boots. He never spoke of receiving any abuse in Scotland. However, we have more contemporary evidence on the treatment black players received in the country. Setting aside the case of Tull, who never actually played football in Scotland, Mark Walters became a pioneer as the first black player to play for Rangers when he was signed by Graeme Souness at the end of 1987. Souness saw only a great footballer and not the colour of his skin. But Mark was a peculiarity or curiosity in Scotland in being a black player. By then, a fair number of black players were already playing in England, though few or none were in the Scottish league. They were the product of immigration through the 1950s and 1960s when their parents set down their roots in the UK. Like most other youngsters, they were raised with a passion for the game.

Many suffered abuse from the terraces, but they became part of the football culture in England long before black players emerged in Scotland.

Walters's debut for Rangers came in the cauldron of an Old Firm match at Parkhead on 2 January 1988. He had to endure a torrent of abuse from the Celtic fans, with bananas and even darts thrown on to the trackside. Similar treatment was inflicted on him just two weeks later when he played against Heart of Midlothian at Tynecastle Park. What is worse is that one of the Hearts players, a former Rangers star, also rounded on him.

Mark recently spoke about his experiences: 'It was intimidating, no two ways about it. I have never experienced anything like it in my life.' He went on to recall that dreadful day and the debris that surrounded him. 'Bananas, a golf ball, even a dart. I am not going to lie – that shocked me. I had two choices – quit Scotland or stick it out. I chose the latter because really that's what guys like me did back then.'

The disgraceful treatment dished out to Walters was not restricted to away fans. Even a small number of Rangers fans were guilty of abuse. Those who were identified were summarily ejected from the stadium and banned from the club for their racist outbursts. Thankfully, all of that died down and Mark is now celebrated as no different from any other former Rangers player, except that he was a special talent. He opened the door to the acceptance of black players in Scotland

and, over the next few years, the country became more multicultural.

We owe Mark Walters a debt of gratitude for his bravery in coming to Scotland and enduring what he had to put up with. It would have been easy for him to give up, but he stuck with it and shut up the racists with his artistry on the field. He certainly paved the way for others to follow in a more tolerant culture in Scottish football. Following Mark's arrival, there was a procession of other black players into the country as they became part of the scene. Perhaps that is why, aside from the particular cases I have highlighted when I was abused, I have never endured any real racial abuse in my time in the country – not just on the field, but off it, too.

I have not been one who frequents pubs and on the occasions when I go to clubs, my visits tend to be for supporters' functions. I would not expect any abuse in that kind of forum, but even in the few pubs I have been to, I have never been conscious of any disrespect based on my colour. Okay, they may have had comments and opinions about my ability, but that is all in the game. Overall, however, I have found Scotland to be a friendly place where, from the very first day I arrived, the people have been welcoming.

As I mentioned, I was conscious when I first arrived in Kirkcaldy that I probably stood out somewhat as the only black person in the town. I suspected that some people may have been whispering as I walked past them, but any racial undertones, if they were ever there, quickly vanished. Even if I had heard any abuse on the streets or on the field, it would not have bothered me much. In Trinidad, although most people were black, name-calling was part of the culture. In my country, you have to 'take talk and give talk'. Dressing rooms, in particular, can be a hard place to survive in if you do not have a thick skin, regardless of colour. I have always just laughed off any comments. It really was water off a duck's back for me. So, it is something that has not bothered me personally, although I know it does effect others.

Any decent person will condemn any kind of racial abuse. Fundamentally, I see it as a question of upbringing. As I said, a child is not born to be racist in any way. It is something that is taught at an early age and there is a message in that from everyone. Parents should naturally want the best for their children in life and freeing them from hate should be the prerogative of good and responsible parenting.

God's word in the Bible (Matthew 22:37–39) is 'love thy neighbour as thyself'. That is how I have lived my life. It is a message that should be considered by anyone drawn to racism in any of its forms.

Chapter 11

God Is My Guide

I AM a Christian and God has carefully laid out the path that I follow. I know where it has taken me up to now, but I do not know what lies ahead. However, I firmly believe that if I pursue the guidance of Jesus Christ, I will fulfil the plan that he has for me and that will be to goodness. As I explained, I have my grandmother to thank for raising me in the Christian faith. It was she who introduced me to Christianity and instructed me to pray to God every day. Had I not gone into her care, I could have become a Shango Baptist, the faith adopted by my mother. She had been attracted to that 'church' as a young lady. Their beliefs were clearly radical and quite fundamental, which caused some concern to my family. If I had remained with her, I would almost certainly have been drawn into the clutches of their followers.

Shango women are generally recognisable in Trinidad. They have strict clothing codes for Shango Baptist events. They wear long skirts and long-sleeved blouses and wrap their hair in headscarves. Men are not bound by codes of dress, but the Orisha priests and chantwells typically wear flowing robes.

The Shango Baptist 'religion' is rooted in Africa and has connections with Spiritual Baptism. A small proportion of the population of Trinidad is descended from Nigerian people of the Yoruba tribe, who were brought to the New World during the slave trade. As the slaves were not allowed to worship their Orisha (the gods in their African traditions), they began to disguise their ceremonies behind Christian services. The Shango Baptists learned to acknowledge Jehovah as the God of man, but they also retained their devotion to the many Orisha spirits, cloaking them behind Christian saints. At their gatherings, the ringing of bells and shouting was fundamental and similar to African rituals which were associated with demonic summoning. During the ceremonies, the Orisha are invited down to possess or 'ride' their specific devotees. The followers must wear and carry the particular colour and implement of the particular Orisha and offer sacrifices – usually animals.

When I arrived in Scotland, my faith strengthened and, as I have said, I have been guided by the Bible. My beliefs are strictly in accordance with the words of Jesus Christ through the New Testament. I believe that Jesus Christ, son of God, died on the cross and then, on the third day, he rose from the dead. He died for our sins. We have all been sinful at some time but, if we repent, Jesus

Christ will pay for our sins. If we do not, then we must pay for them and be cast to hell.

As I have explained, my place of worship is the Zion Praise Centre in Kirkcaldy. It is a Pentecostal Church with its beliefs rooted in Jesus Christ and the Holy Spirit. The scripture says that 'for those who are led by the spirit of God are the children of God'.

Belief in the Bible is the tenet that is central to the church. It guides me in my life and everything we do in the church is directed by what is written. If the Old Testament established the laws for mankind, then the New Testament brings out the word of Jesus Christ in interpreting these laws. If you live by the laws of the Old Testament, then you live by the word of Jesus Christ in the New Testament. Christ is the guiding light and my whole being – my health, fitness, strength and my body were created by God. It is through him that we are here. But for the grace of God, there would not have been a Marvin Andrews.

In the church, we provide a warm and welcoming place for people to come to, share their beliefs and rejoice in the word of God. We are audible, singing with tambourines and drums as accompaniment, although we do not have a choir. Besides singing, we say prayers, spending anything from an hour to a couple of hours or so in the services. The services are generally based upon readings from the Bible, which we relate to the issues in people's lives or current affairs. We talk about the problems in life and sometimes the parishioners will want to chat about their own personal problems on a one-to-one basis. We help each other in guidance, drawing our advice from the Bible. We never advocate our own beliefs, but simply relate what is written. I spend most of my spare time there, as it provides me with an opportunity to sit with others who share my beliefs. It is a happy and comforting place to be.

Nowadays, our numbers are smaller than they once were, which reflects the dwindling support for churches in Scotland. The longer I have lived in Scotland, the more I recognise what a powerful role it once played in the spread of Christianity. The 16th-century leader of the Reformation, John Knox, who travelled across Europe meeting church modernists, was the founder of Presbyterianism in Scotland. The 19th-century missionary and explorer David Livingstone was born and raised in Blantyre. In his travels to Africa through the 1840s to the 1870s, he spread the gospel, carrying the word of God throughout the continent. These were powerful men of God from a past era when the church was important to the lives of people in Scotland. There were many others of that ilk in the country.

Now, I look around and see many churches in every town, with seemingly one on every corner. Not so long ago, they were all well attended, but now many have closed and have been converted into homes and clubs. It is not an issue solely in Scotland, but it is a worldwide trend, as people become more and more ungodly. It is a sign of the times that many of the older people, who were once the guardians of their faith and supporters of the church, died without passing on that commitment to their children. Where once most people felt a need go to go church, it is no longer the case. I recognise that most people continue with their belief in God, but do not feel it necessary to attend church.

For some, the weakening of their faith has come from a belief that they cannot commit to God and enjoy themselves in life, as if the two were incompatible. It is not true, of course. I realise, too, that people have questioned the Bible, especially since it was written several hundred years after the events it portrays. Some say that it was written by man, not God. Then again, the laws of the country were written by man and we adhere to them without question. In the case of the Bible, it is my belief that it was written by men who were inspired and directed by God to put into print his word.

In John 15:12, Jesus said: 'Love one another as I have loved you.' I have always been there for my friends and family. I am regularly contacted by people who face difficult situations in their lives, asking me to offer prayers to help them. At Ibrox, I had quiet conversations with some of my team-mates when they sought some help from above. Fernando Ricksen was one that I spoke with many times about Christianity. I found it really heartbreaking that a terrible disease debilitated him and turned him into the complete opposite of what he really was – a fun and fit guy. In the latter stages when I talked to him, he found it physically difficult to respond. I sent a video message to him and I said that God can make him well, but it wasn't to be. Although I was there through much of his deterioration, I sadly never got the chance to get to see him much in his final days. He had a circle of friends around him who were very protective and latterly that barrier seemed impenetrable.

That was not the case with Andy Goram, 'The Goalie'. Just a day or so before he died, he was suffering and finding difficulty with breathing. I had a sense from God that I had to visit Andy and I went to see him at his bedside. We had a quiet, private chat and I decided that I would lead him to the path of God. There is no repentance in a grave, so I asked him to lie back and to ask God to forgive him for all his wrongdoings, repeating the words I gave him. He joined me quietly in prayer and his son, Danny, was with us. It was a very private moment and the details of what was said will remain with me. I knew that he was near the end and, after we had prayed, I told him: 'Do not worry – everything will be all right.' A sense of calm came over him as he lay back on his pillow then fell asleep. I think he had a sense of peace and I believe he passed away serenely a day or so later. I had never played football with Andy, except in charity testimonial matches, but I did get quite close to him. He was a good friend and it was sad to see him slip away.

Often, I will receive messages from others through social media asking me to help in prayers when times are tough for them. That is probably why I found it quite a natural progression in my life to assist at Pastor Joe's church. I typically spend three days a week there, attending every Wednesday, Friday and Sunday. When the pastor is unavailable, I take services, too. As a Pentecostal church, our beliefs are evangelical, emphasising direct experience of God through baptism with the Holy Spirit. To us, the Bible is inerrant. We believe the repentance of individuals will lead them to accepting Jesus Christ as their personal lord and saviour.

Our church is welcoming to people from all sorts of backgrounds, some coming with physical, emotional or financial problems. We pray with them for God's help. Through the church and with the power of prayer, I have been privileged to see what faith can provide, relieving people from their darkest days. I was officiating at a wedding a couple of years ago and I was introduced to a man who had terminal cancer, with a prognosis of just two weeks to live. I was asked to pray for him and he went on to survive for two years. Then there was a woman who lost her husband and four children, all aged under four, in a house fire. Only her six-year-old daughter survived, because she was at school.

She was introduced to Paster Joe and then I spoke with her, assuring her that God would see that her children would have a place in heaven. We comforted her, showing her that she could turn her life around and that there was a way forward. Eventually, as she and her little daughter came to Bible classes, she got stronger in her beliefs and her trust in God. Eventually, she was baptised. She gained comfort by coming to church and got her life back on track, regaining peace and joy.

Some people may find it hard to understand how such a terrible thing can happen, but John 10:10 says: 'The thief comes only to steal and kill and destroy; I have come that they may have life and have it to the full.' In this context, 'thief' is the Devil (or Satan), who creates such tragedy and despair, but God is the restorer and repairer of life.

* * *

When I was ordained in September 2006, people came to the church because of my fame. You may recall how I explained that I was a shy child, but the confidence I have gained from playing football enables me to stand in front of a congregation and lead the spiritual guidance. Indeed, when I first went along to the church with Anthony Rougier, I was terrified and even felt self-conscious singing and clapping. It was intimidating at first when I took the sermon, because I was conscious that I was standing there and that people were awaiting my words. Some may have been looking for spiritual guidance. Eventually, I learned that I should trust in God and the words came freely. Now, I am happy to stand up in front of any congregation in any church and confidently deliver a sermon.

I rarely prepare any sermon, instead asking God to give me guidance on what I should speak about in each service. He will give me the subject and the words and I open my heart to allow the right message to be conveyed. Often, one of the congregation will come forward afterwards to say that my words resonated with them in the problems they were facing. Everything I deliver in a sermon can be illustrated as being the word of God or Jesus Christ.

I am fortunate in that I have memorised the Bible, so the words of the scriptures come readily to me. I hope that each time I deliver my sermon there is an answer there for at least one of the congregation. It is common for people to have relationship problems and these often arise through a man or woman placing trust in their partner. It is an inevitability because, although everyone will base their relationship on trust in their partner, the Lord says: 'Blessed is the man or woman who puts their trust in God.'

Everyone will have their own views and strength of faith, if they have any. I have never imposed my beliefs on others except when they open up the discussions or seek guidance from me. Obviously, as a football player, I encountered players of different faiths. In the Trinidad and Tobago national team, we had some players who were non-Christian, but we all prayed together. It is a question of respect, but if any non-Christians wanted to open up the debate on my beliefs, I would always be ready to do so for those who wanted to learn about Jesus Christ or the Bible. I see myself as someone who projects the love of God and his word.

I am fortunate that the career and profile I have through football has created the platform for me to proclaim the gospel. It was God who put me in this arena as a professional footballer, to talk about Jesus Christ to thousands of people who have never heard his words. Football is important to so many people and to have played with such a big club as Rangers widens the scope of those who may be interested in my thoughts and beliefs in God. In Scottish football, religion was often caught up in the Catholic-Protestant thing, but the discussions never deliberated upon God. Hopefully, I have been able to impact on that and allow people to appreciate and understand the words of Jesus Christ without getting caught up in religious conflicts. The Lord said 'go to all the world and preach the good news', which is what I do. We live in a society where bad news travels faster than good news, so I have a duty to go out and relay the message of Jesus Christ. I really believe that my coming to Scotland was a mission and I have answered that calling at a time when many people may have turned their backs on God.

The stories surrounding my knee and then the miracle of Helicopter Sunday elevated many people's interests in my beliefs. Those iconic words of 'keep believing' were probably little more than a sideshow to many fans and even to some players at the time. When the title win came to pass in what seemed unlikely circumstances, some began to wonder – there may be something in all of this. In that regard, the importance of that day in Edinburgh in May 2005 cannot be underestimated in terms of projecting the message. While many Rangers fans were believers before that momentous day, there were also some who were either wavering or did not carry any beliefs. They watched and saw my apparent miraculous recovery from my knee injury, then saw Rangers go on to win the title in such dramatic circumstances. Some people have said to me that these events changed the way they think. I hope that some have been drawn to reflect on their own faith. Perhaps they will see and consider what God can bring to their lives.

Of course, it was not just the fans who were stunned by the turn of the events in those weeks leading up to Helicopter Sunday. For several weeks, my stock answer to my team-mates who queried whether we would win the title was the same – 'keep believing'. By then, the players were well adjusted to the strength of my faith and showed some curiosity and interest in my beliefs. Football dressing rooms can be difficult environments, given the emotions of training and playing matches at high levels and all the associated pressures. It can be a hard place for the weak to survive in, so my faith caused some confusion for some. Discussions on God are not commonplace in that forum. At Ibrox, though, rather than facing disdain, I found many of my team-mates were open to embrace my beliefs, even if they found them hard to understand at times.

After we won the title, the players involved stood back and reflected on what had happened. In my experience, most footballers believe in God, but in a reserved manner. Certainly, after these events, some of my team-mates became more open about their own beliefs. There were times when I would have nice one-to-one conversations with the likes of Barry Ferguson, who was keen to explore my beliefs and reflect on his own. The players may not have been certain why these things happened, but many realised that there was a higher being directing things. For those who had no belief in God, it raised the possibility in their own minds that perhaps there was a superior driving force in life.

After Helicopter Sunday, the words 'keep believing' characterised me. While I may have been a caricature of faith at one time, people stopped in their tracks after the events of that day. Now, whenever anyone sees me, their thoughts tend to revolve around that phrase. The fundamentals of those words are in Mark 9:23, in which Jesus said: 'If you can believe, all things are possible to him/her that believes.'

Kit man Jimmy Bell, now sadly deceased, was one who used to chat with me quite often, making playful jokes about my beliefs. He had a great love for his grandson and would tell me of his plans for the coming week with him. We would have a chat around that, but I was often heartened when he asked me to say a prayer for the wee man. Regrettably, he would not see him grow up, but Jimmy's love for him was unquestionable and it was heartening that he wanted me to pray to God for him.

I have always played out the Bible through my behaviour, which might not always have been in harmony with the other players. Even if we lost a match at the weekend, I would come into the dressing room on Monday morning full of the joys of spring, while many of the players would be moping around. 'How can you be so bubbly when we lost?' they would ask. My belief is that, quite simply, there is nothing I can do about the past, so now I have to look forward to the future. It might have been quite radical for some to accept, but many of my team-mates would chat with me about God and they all respected my faith.

Barry used to always puzzle over how I was so happy. In contrast, he was the kind of guy who was angry with the world all the time. He would fall out with ten people before he even got to training! I used to tell him to enjoy life and that I was happy because I could rejoice at being alive. I used to say to him: 'Why should you be so angry? You have it all – wonderful ability on the field, you are playing for the club that you love, you are adored by thousands of fans and you have all the fame that comes with it.' It resonated with Barry and some time later, he took me aside and said: 'I now understand what you were saying to me.' Now Barry is a completely different character – much more relaxed and contented. I am not saying that he is a born-again Christian, but he obviously reflected on his life and has become a much better person for it.

When I was writing this book, I was asked to consider who might write the foreword. For me, there could only be one person and that was Barry. That is how highly I value our relationship and how much I respect him, not only as a footballer, but as a human being.

I used to have light-hearted conversations with my former team-mate Dado Prso, who showed a lot of interest in my beliefs. We used to debate the origins of life from a biblical sense. He would say: 'If I go to bed with my wife and we make love, then a child is produced from my sperm and her egg. The baby is considered to be mine, or ours. It is a product of our hard work!' But I would always counter that children were a blessing from God. Psalm 127:3 says: 'Children are a gift from the Lord; they are a reward from him.'

I would say that he created you – your lungs, your heart, your brain, indeed your whole body, and he also created your child. Our chats were always fun, but they came from Dado's genuine curiosity in my beliefs. We ran through the same debate countless times and even though I may never have convinced him, it was heartening that he was debating it all. As I say, I never imposed my beliefs on anyone in these circumstances.

It is not sufficient to read the Bible and have a strong belief in its words, because actions must speak louder than the written word. We have a basic duty to live our lives in a good way and I try to project the Bible through the way I lead my life. Not that I have always been fully aware of its contents. When I first read the Bible, I did not understand it all. It was only through going to church that I discovered what the written texts meant and how they may be interpreted. The church is a forum which provides instruction on the scriptures. When I read the Bible in church, I try to relate it to modern society and life. Just as you might buy an appliance, which typically comes with an instruction manual, the Bible is the manual for mankind. I believe that, in modern life, everything can be related back to the Bible, which is why it provides good guidance for people. There is a story in it for everyone and every situation that anyone might face.

If that suggests that I am wholly righteous, I have to say that it was not always so. When I was a teenager back in Trinidad, I was exposed to all of the vices that can lead youngsters down the wrong path. It is so easy in these circumstances to be influenced by the words of your friends and take a path that may lead to ruin. I recall one occasion, at 15 years of age, when things could have gone disastrously wrong for me. I was down at the market in San Juan when one of my friends handed me a bag of crack cocaine and asked me to stick it down my trousers. I did not think and reacted immediately, shoving it beneath my waistband. Just then, two police officers came slowly walking towards me. My 'friend' must have seen the police coming, prompting him to pass it to me. I was terrified at being discovered and the consequences of being caught with the drugs. I had dreams of being a professional footballer, but this could have destroyed everything. If I had been caught, I might still have been in jail with the amount that was in that bag.

As it turned out, the police walked past and I could quickly hand the bag back, but I never went near that market again. On another occasion, I got involved in a drinking session and downed a lot of vodka. My head was spinning and I was as sick as a dog. It was enough to prevent me ever getting drunk again. Playing cards and gambling in school was not out of bounds either at that time. However, for all these lapses in judgement in getting involved in some crazy things, I never did anything that could be judged criminal or really bad. It was all part of growing up and the learning process of youth, but certainly I was not living a life that would be considered righteous at that time.

Of course, the incident in the market was also a key point in my growing up, but the major turning point or sense of enlightenment came when I sustained the injury to my pelvis shortly after arriving in Scotland. The circumstances opened the door to my experience of healing through prayer and the strength of my faith, which had been revitalised when I visited the church. From then, I was a born-again Christian and began to live my life in a more wholesome way. I do not profess myself to be perfect, but I try to live my life in a good way. I treat others the way I want to be treated. For all that is written in the Bible, my actions speak louder than the words that are written there. I try to be the best I can be and to lead a life that reflects my beliefs in the Bible.

When I sustained the injury to my knee, there were lots of things for me to consider. If I had an operation, I would miss the league run-in with Rangers and the World Cup finals with Trinidad and Tobago. That evening, when I ran it through my mind, I prayed to God to help me make the right decision. When I woke up the next day, everything was so clear in my mind. I knew that I had to put my trust in God to heal me. Whether it can be argued it was the strength of my quad muscles or any other physical condition that allowed me to play, the guidance I received from the Lord was that I did not need an operation at that time and so it was to be.

The decision I should make was absolutely clear in my mind – God had spoken to me. I did not disregard the medical opinion and I am not telling people to ignore their doctor's advice, but I took God's advice that I should keep believing and trusting in him. Through the power of my faith, I believe that I overcame my injury through spiritual healing. The Bible tells us of the healing that

Jesus performed by miraculous means. He healed those who were sick and also those who were sinners, his healing being through repentance. That is why he is known as the 'Great Physician'.

It may sound like I had blind faith, especially considering that years later I did go for an operation, but things are much more complex than that. Then I put my faith in the specialists who operated on my knee. The time was right for me to go through medical procedures. In our church, we strongly believe in divine healing, but we also believe in medicine and doctors. Doctors, dentists and physiotherapists, like people in every other profession, reach their level of specialism because they are following the path God laid out for them. When I underwent the operation, I placed my faith in the surgeons, but spiritual faith is different.

Aside from the celebrated impact of faith on my injury, I have always relied on God's guidance in all my major life decisions. When I was approached to join Dundee United, I would miss a chance of playing in the League Cup Final with Livingston, of course, but I needed the clouds to be removed from my mind. I prayed to God to lead me to the right path and, again, the next morning I awoke with the clarity that I should not go to Tannadice.

If my faith has guided me on the path of life, it has also given me strength in my character. It has allowed me to deal with all of life's challenges to the extent that I am comfortable in most circumstances that I encounter.

Probably my favourite verse in the Bible is from Mark 11:22. It reads: 'Have faith in God. Truly, I say to you, whoever says to this mountain "Be taken up and thrown into the sea" and does not doubt in his heart, but believes that what he says will come to pass, it will be done for him.' Essentially, it outlines how to deal with problems (mountains). If you toss them aside and believe, then your wishes will be fulfilled. That is, if you walk with Jesus, you will overcome your problems.

It is by acknowledging these words that I do not become overly preoccupied by life's problems. Of course, things do not always work out the way we want. Whenever things have gone wrong in my life, I realise that it is all part of God's plan for me. In John 16:33, Jesus Christ said: 'In this world you will have troubles, but be of good cheer, I have overcome the world.' Then, in Romans 8:28, the scripture says: 'All things work together for good for the man or woman who loves God.' Nothing good in life comes easy, as the pain a woman suffers in childbirth illustrates, but at the end she is joyous because she has delivered a beautiful baby. I overcome my problems by placing my faith in Jesus Christ that things will work out for the better, or for good, according to the plan or purpose that God has for my life. The only people with no problems are in the cemetery. God can use your troubles to help mould you into the man or woman he created you to be on this earth. When you go through difficult times, do not be depressed – rejoice because, with faith and trust in God, it is through our most difficult times that greatness is born. Many people believe that they cannot enjoy their life if they have problems, but the scripture tells us: 'He/she who calls on God, shall be answered by him and he shall be with them in times of trouble.'

I am acutely aware that the source of many problems in the world are born from the Devil. There are many people who do not believe in the Devil or Satan, but his work can be seen everywhere in everyday life. I am always wary to counter any attempt that the Devil may have to enter my life.

The most important parts of the body are the 'heart' or mind and mouth. Everything that we do or say originates from the heart or mind. If you love someone, we say you love them with your heart. If you are afraid, the fear comes from your heart. Similarly, if we speak in anger or talk of hate, it comes from the heart. When anyone speaks ill of someone, or swears for example, it does not originate from their mouth. It comes from their heart and reflects the Devil's work. Out of the heart, the mouth speaks. A good man brings good things out of the good stored up in him and an evil man brings evil things out of the evil stored up in him. Your words show what is in your heart. In the case of evil words, I believe that this is the Devil exercising control on a person. It is how he works. So, I resist all hate and negative words. I abhor negativity, so I am like a scanner against negative words because the scripture says (Proverbs 18:21): 'The tongue has the power of life and death, and those who love it will eat its fruit.'

Even on the football field, which is a passionate environment, I would resist retaliation and swearing because I allow God to be in control of me. For the same reason, I never argued with referees, although I have to admit that I have been shown a red card, but for a bad challenge which was not made in malice.

Over the years, most media coverage about me has been positive, but there was once a story that broke that created a bit of controversy – my views on homosexuality. Actually, the circumstances surrounding the story were not entirely accurate, but it is as well to set the record straight here. I have absolutely no problem with homosexual people, just as I do not have any problems with those who like a drink or smoke. I respect every man and woman's choice on how they choose to live their life, because choice is the greatest thing that God has given to mankind (Deuteronomy 30:19). The main issue for me is that the Bible prohibits the act of homosexuality and I believe the Bible. Leviticus 18:22 says: 'You shall not lie with a male as with a woman; it is an abomination.' However, the personal lives of others are their business and not mine.

I enjoy speaking with people, but I have also felt that I have a particular resonance with youngsters. I feel that I can particularly express the message of God to them and that they are generally receptive. With the difficult upbringing I had in Trinidad, I can empathise with many young people and the pressures they face in modern life. I have always had this desire to see them succeed, probably at least in part because of the difficulties I faced at their age. I have a certain rapport that enables me to engage quite easily with the kids, enabling me to speak quite freely with them. Some can drift in life, believing they have little to offer society, but God gave everyone an ability, a gift, a passion and a way to lead their lives productively. It is up to youngsters to pursue that talent, uncovering the life that brings them happiness.

Everyone was born for a purpose in life and we should all strive to find that purpose. It is an issue of being careful about who your friends are, because it is often difficult to say 'no' to them. Life is about making the right choices and then following the path that leads to fulfilment. That is the message I like to convey to them.

Besides youngsters, I have been fortunate that people feel comfortable telling me their problems, probably because I am a good listener. I am humbled by that because it implies that they trust me. Some have said that they feel comfortable in talking with me. It is possibly because I treat everyone as an equal. It does not matter what background they have or what problems that they are enduring, I will always have time to speak. I never talk down to or look down on anyone.

At Ibrox, for example, whenever I meet the staff cleaning the rooms or serving at the tables, I will always have a chat to find out how they are. If they are still at college, I like to find out how they are doing with their studies. Whether they are the poorest people in the stadium or the richest, it matters not to me. I believe that everyone is facing some battle or problems, regardless of their circumstances. Essentially, we do not know how people are and what problems they are going through. It is good to chat and offer some support and encouragement.

Even if they have sinned, I will sit with them. The gospels tell us that Jesus regularly ate with sinners, including prostitutes and tax collectors. He did not do so to share nourishment, but he believed that the meal created the forum in which he could turn them back to God.

Given the strength of my faith, some have queried why I played football on the Sabbath. Eric Liddell, an athlete who was featured in the movie *Chariots of Fire*, famously withdrew from the qualifying heats for his strongest event, the 100m, at the 1924 Paris Olympic Games because they were scheduled for a Sunday. In contrast, I have never had a problem in playing or doing anything else on a Sunday because nowhere does it say in the Bible that you cannot. It is all a matter of interpretation, which is the substance of religion, not the Bible. People interpret the seventh day as Sunday, but who even can say that? In any case, every day is the Sabbath for me. I pray each day and read the Bible.

By now, you will understand that I place so much faith in the Lord and he guides me through my life. No matter that football has brought me a good life, with financial stability, I am nothing without God in my life. God has given me the ability to earn everything I have achieved in life. I lead my life through the word of God. It is a good way to live.

Chapter 12

Life after Football

WITH MY professional football career over, I can concentrate more on my church activities, my work as an ordained pastor and on more peripheral football matters. I have also found that I built quite a gathering of fans on social media, which I found particularly useful in the periods of lockdown during the Covid pandemic. I found Twitter provided an opportunity to send out short inspirational messages and videos of my singing!

I am not a fabulous singer, but I am a cheery guy; I like to laugh, have fun and enjoy life. Anyone who knows me will verify that I am always laughing. One day I thought I would sing a song and put it on Twitter (now known as X), just for a laugh. I never thought I would get such a response. It was unbelievable. I used to go down to my car, which was my makeshift recording studio. I would learn the lyrics of a song that was topical and then go for it.

I do not imagine that I would make any TV talent show, but if I was putting a smile on somebody's face, then my job was done. They might be in a bad place, they might be going through a difficult time in their life, but hopefully my videos brought a little cheer to their lives. I always found it funny reading the comments from people when these little videos went viral.

They became so popular that people would call out on the street to ask what my next song would be. Among my favourite 'hits' were 'Wanna Be Startin' Somethin'', 'Live it Up', 'Don't Worry' … and the catalogue goes on. The Rangers songs like 'Four Lads Had a Dream' were also popular. It is all a bit of fun and now, when I do gigs at supporters' functions and the like, I am often asked to sing. I have even been called to do karaoke, but in the strangest of circumstances. When the musical play *The Journey Back* came to the Armadillo in Glasgow in February 2024, I had a bit part on stage, singing to more than 3,000 people. The play features the most recent period of Rangers' history, through the eyes of a father and son on the journey to success and stability. Part of it is set in a bar and when the karaoke starts, they call for Marvin. I then step on to the stage to the acclamation of the crowd, launching the entire theatre off on the singing! It was great fun, but who would believe that this once shy wee lad from Trinidad would end up on stage singing in front of thousands.

Rangers have a fanzone which is popular on matchdays and when we had pop artist Callum Beattie on stage, high on the gantry, I got the chance to sing while he played guitar to accompany me. It was a great experience, although I am not quite ready to switch careers. My devotion remains with the Bible and the church.

Away from the microphone, I get enormous satisfaction in helping people whenever I can. I am often approached by strangers in need of spiritual advice and I am always happy to offer any guidance that I can. This is another area in which my faith can help to shape my life and that of others. It may involve pointing out chapters in the Bible that individuals can read, giving them the direction they need for the particular situation they face. I get different requests from people from all walks of life because they know the strength of the faith that I have in Jesus Christ.

Increasingly, I have also been asked to attend Christian gatherings to talk about my faith. Recently, I was invited to the Isle of Skye to speak to a gathering at Portree High School. There were more than 100 in attendance, of various ages. I spoke about my life in football, but also of my beliefs. The evening, which was organised by a number of local churches, went well and they have invited me to return and take part in a charity match.

On another occasion fairly recently, I travelled up to Thurso with some of the Rangers coaches to put more than 100 local youngsters through their paces. It was part of an event run by Thurso Football Academy and the local schools for the benefit of kids aged from two to

15. I had to leave at 3am to be there in time, but it was a worthwhile exercise.

One of the joys of being ordained is being able to bring people together in holy matrimony and I have officiated at several weddings. In fact, now I have a lengthy waiting list extending over 18 months. Many of these were held inside Ibrox and involved fervent fans. In March 2018, I flew back to Trinidad to officiate at the marriage of my close friend and former team-mate Jason Scotland and his wife, Debbi O'Rourke. They tied the knot at Drew Manor on the Caribbean island, close to where both Jason and I grew up in San Juan. We have known each other since we were teenagers and we played in the Trinidad and Tobago team together. That friendship remains and I often visit them in Glasgow, where the happy couple settled.

It was an honour to be asked and it is a special feeling to do your best friend's wedding. The ceremony itself was all close family and friends. It was really beautiful. Debbi's family were pleased to have me officiate because they are all Rangers diehards.

Jason and Debbi's wedding was not the first I have carried out for a former player. In 2015, I officiated at the wedding between my ex-team-mate Nach Novo and Donna Clark. Sadly, they are no longer together, but it was a lovely wedding.

I have officiated at some funerals, but generally only when they have involved close friends. I have also done some christenings but, again, these have typically been for people I am well acquainted with. My clerical work largely revolves around my church and that is where I can relay the words of the Bible.

In more recent times, I have worked as a hospitality ambassador at Rangers Football Club. On matchdays, I go along to Ibrox and rotate around the corporate suites, meeting guests and sharing their memories of my time as a player at the club. It helps keep me in touch with the game and also some of the former players who perform similar roles. Alex Rae, who is now on the backroom staff at Ibrox, Barry Ferguson, Bob Malcolm and Craig Moore, all former team-mates, share the matchday duties with me. Others in our group of former players include Colin Stein, Willie Johnston, Willie Henderson, Jonatan Johansson, Gordon Durie, Alex MacDonald and Alan McLaren. It is great to keep that old dressing-room humour going when we meet up.

It is wonderful being involved again at Rangers, where I enjoyed my greatest time in football. To be part of it all and recognised as a former player is a huge honour. It gives me enormous satisfaction and nowadays I spend a lot of time helping out the club in many roles, interfacing with fans and corporate clients.

Some days I sit quietly and reflect on my life journey and I am so thankful for the path God has guided me along. I have come a long way since my formative years in San Juan and, while there have been twists and turns,

I would not change any part of it at all. I look forward with hope and faith to the road ahead – following, as I will, in the words of the Lord.

Marvin Andrews

Club and Individual Honours

This is a summary of my playing career as drawn from club records and other sources.

Livingston:	Scottish First Division	2000/01
	Scottish League Cup	2004
Rangers:	Scottish Premier League	2004/05
Raith Rovers:	Scottish Second Division	2008/09

Trinidad and Tobago:	Caribbean Cup	1999, 2001

Raith Rovers Player of the Year	2000
Livingston Player of the Year	2003, 2004
Rangers Players' Player of the Year	2005
Chaconia Medal (World Cup squad) Gold Class	2006
Raith Rovers Hall of Fame	2016

Statistics

Team	*Period*	*Appearances*	*Goals*
Trinidad & Tobago	1996–2009	**102**	**10**
ECM Motown	1992–1994	-	-
San Juan Jabloteh	1995–96	-	-
Malta Carib Alcons	1996–97	-	-
Raith Rovers	1997–00, 2006–08, 2009	145	14
Livingston	2000–04	119	8
Rangers	2004–06	75	8
Hamilton Academical	2009–10	2	0
Queen of the South (loan)	2009–10	2	0
Queen of the South	2010	4	0
Wrexham	2010–11	30	2
Kirkintilloch Rob Roy	2011–12	5	0
Albion Rovers	2013	17	2
Forfar Athletic	2013–14	18	0
Elgin City	2014–15	17	3
Montrose	2015	12	2
Clyde	2015–16	16	1
TOTAL		**462**	**40**